WORLD
HISTORY SERIES ■ ■ ■

The California
Gold Rush

Titles in the World History Series

WORLD HISTORY SERIES ■■■

The California Gold Rush

by
Tom Ito

Lucent Books, P.O. Box 289011, San Diego, CA 92198-9011

Library of Congress Cataloging-in-Publication Data

Ito, Tom.
    The California gold rush / by Tom Ito.
      p. cm.—(World history series)
    Includes bibliographical references (p.   ) and index.
    Summary: Discusses the events surrounding the
nineteenth-century gold rush in California, the lifestyle of
miners, and the phenomena of boom towns and ghost towns.
    ISBN 1-56006-293-2 (alk. paper)
    1. California—Gold discoveries—Juvenile literature.
2. Gold mines and mining—California—History—19th
century—Juvenile literature.   [1. California—Gold
discoveries.   2. Gold mines and mining—California—
History—19th century.]   I.Title.   II. Series.
F865.I56   1997
979.4'04—dc20   96-26354
                                                 CIP
                                                 AC

Copyright 1997 by Lucent Books, Inc., P.O. Box 289011,
San Diego, California 92198-9011

Printed in the U.S.A.

Contents

Foreword

Each year on the first day of school, nearly every history teacher faces the task of explaining why his or her students should study history. One logical answer to this question is that exploring what happened in our past explains how the things we often take for granted—our customs, ideas, and institutions—came to be. As statesman and historian Winston Churchill put it, "Every nation or group of nations has its own tale to tell. Knowledge of the trials and struggles is necessary to all who would comprehend the problems, perils, challenges, and opportunities which confront us today." Thus, a study of history puts modern ideas and institutions in perspective. For example, though the founders of the United States were talented and creative thinkers, they clearly did not invent the concept of democracy. Instead, they adapted some democratic ideas that had originated in ancient Greece and with which the Romans, the British, and others had experimented. An exploration of these cultures, then, reveals their very real connection to us through institutions that continue to shape our daily lives.

Another reason often given for studying history is the idea that lessons exist in the past from which contemporary societies can benefit and learn. This idea, although controversial, has always been an intriguing one for historians. Those that agree that society can benefit from the past often quote philosopher George Santayana's famous statement, "Those who cannot remember the past are condemned to repeat it." Historians who ascribe to Santayana's philosophy believe that, for example, studying the events that led up to the major world wars or other significant historical events would allow society to chart a different and more favorable course in the future.

Just as difficult as convincing students to realize the importance of studying history is the search for useful and interesting supplementary materials that present historical events in a context that can be easily understood. The volumes in Lucent Books' World History Series attempt to present a broad, balanced, and penetrating view of the march of history. Ancient Egypt's important wars and rulers, for example, are presented against the rich and colorful backdrop of Egyptian religious, social, and cultural developments. The series engages the reader by enhancing historical events with these cultural contexts. For example, in *Ancient Greece*, the text covers the role of women in that society. Slavery is discussed in *The Roman Empire*, as well as how slaves earned their freedom. The numerous and varied aspects of everyday life in these and other societies are explored in each volume of the series. Additionally, the series covers the major political, cultural, and philosophical ideas as the torch of civilization is passed from ancient Mesopotamia and Egypt, through Greece, Rome, Medieval Europe, and other world cultures, to the modern day.

The material in the series is formatted in a thorough, precise, and organized manner. Each volume offers the reader a comprehensive and clearly written overview of an important historical event or period. The topic under discussion is placed in a broad historical context. For example, *The Italian Renaissance* begins with a discussion of the High Middle Ages and the loss of central control that allowed certain Italian cities to develop artistically. The book ends by looking forward to the Reformation and interpreting the societal changes that grew out of the Renaissance. Thus, students are not only involved in an historical era, but also enveloped by the events leading up to that era and the events following it.

One important and unique feature in the World History Series is the primary and secondary source quotations that richly supplement each volume. These quotes are useful in a number of ways. First, they allow students access to sources they would not normally be exposed to because of the difficulty and obscurity of the original source. The quotations range from interesting anecdotes to farsighted cultural perspectives and are drawn from historical witnesses both past and present. Second, the quotes demonstrate how and where historians themselves derive their information on the past as they strive to reach a consensus on historical events. Lastly, all of the quotes are footnoted, familiarizing students with the citation process and allowing them to verify quotes and/or look up the original source if the quote piques their interest.

Finally, the books in the World History Series provide a detailed launching point for further research. Each book contains a bibliography specifically geared toward student research. A second, annotated bibliography introduces students to all the sources the author consulted when compiling the book. A chronology of important dates gives students an overview, at a glance, of the topic covered. Where applicable, a glossary of terms is included.

In short, the series is designed not only to acquaint readers with the basics of history, but also to make them aware that their lives are a part of an ongoing human saga. Perhaps they will then come to the same realization as famed historian Arnold Toynbee. In his monumental work, *A Study of History*, he wrote about becoming aware of history flowing through him in a mighty current, and of his own life "welling like a wave in the flow of this vast tide."

Important Dates in the History of the California Gold Rush

1848	1849	1852	1853	1856	1859

1848

January 24: James Marshall discovers gold at Sutter's sawmill at Coloma; mid-April: Sam Brannan announces news of gold discovery in San Francisco; July 4: John Bidwell discovers rich gold strike at Bidwell's Bar; August 17: Colonel R. B. Mason, military governor of California, sends report of gold discovery to Washington, D.C., along with gold samples; community of Yerba Buena renamed San Francisco.

1849

Gold rush attracts worldwide immigration to California; San Francisco becomes major port of entry of the gold rush; population of Sacramento grows to twelve thousand as Argonauts flock to the settlement.

1852

French prospector Chabot develops method of washing gold-bearing ore with a hose; dwindling placer deposits lead to development of more sophisticated mining methods; 108 mills estimated to be in operation in the goldfields.

1853

Population in goldfields reaches an estimated one hundred thousand; gold production estimated at sixty-seven million dollars; bandit alleged to be Joaquin Murieta killed by Harry Love and company of twenty rangers.

1856

John Butterfield founds first overland mail stage service across the United States to California.

1859

Discovery of silver in Nevada triggers great stampede and marks the end of the California gold rush; approximately two million dollars in gold mined in California since Marshall's discovery.

A World-Shaking Discovery

The discovery of gold at Sutter's Mill in 1848 dramatically influenced California history and generated tremendous excitement throughout the world. At the time of the discovery California was an undeveloped province under U.S. control, though not yet officially declared an American territory, with a population of a few thou-

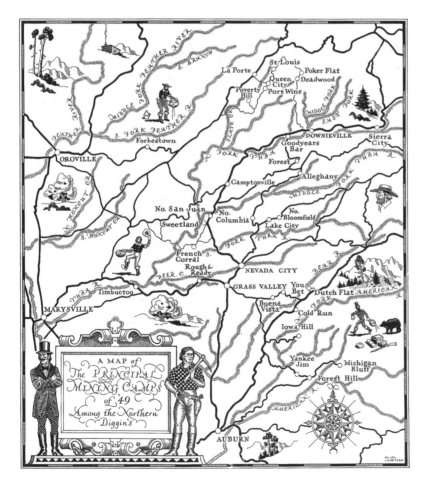

The lure of gold and adventure brought hordes of prospectors into California during the late 1840s. This map reveals the number of mining camps that prospectors formed wherever gold had been discovered.

News of gold spread swiftly, and the dream of striking it rich lured fortune seekers to the goldfields. Here, prospectors comb for gold in the Sierra foothills.

sand. As news of the discovery spread, however, the number of fortune seekers who rushed to the former Mexican territory was estimated to be as many as a half million people.

Gold fever spread throughout the United States and eventually throughout the world. Reacting to newspaper stories describing incredible fortunes of gold waiting to be claimed in the foothills of the Sierra Nevada, where the first nuggets had been found, farmers abandoned their crops, tellers and clerks their jobs, and sailors their ships to join in the eager stampede west. The gold rush included masses of immigrants from Europe, Chile, Peru, China, and other foreign lands as well. As hordes of prospectors continued to seek

out the goldfields, mining camps and communities called boomtowns sprang up and rapidly spread throughout gold country.

California's goldfields proved to be fabulously rich with the precious metal. Although records of the time vary, estimates of gold production for 1848 alone were as high as ten million dollars. By 1852, the peak of the gold rush, estimates of gold mined from the goldfields had climbed to eighty-one million dollars.

For the six years following the first discovery, prospectors ranged through the Sierra foothills seeking the yellow metal in riverbeds, valleys, ravines, and mountainsides. These miners became known as Argonauts, after the men who followed the Greek mythological hero, Jason, in search of the Golden Fleece. Although these nineteenth-century Argonauts had been drawn west originally in search of gold and adventure, many would remain in California and make significant contributions to the development of the state.

Economic Prosperity

Gold rush miners' demand for supplies and provisions stimulated a vigorous commerce among merchants. Blacksmith shops, ferry services, general stores, restaurants, and more flourished as a result of the tremendous population growth stimulated by the gold rush. These and other businesses, including farming, would combine to help build California into one of the most economically prosperous states in the nation.

Despite the abundance of gold, few of the thousands of people who prospected or mined became wealthy. Although fortunate exceptions like John Bidwell and John and Daniel Murphy made immense fortunes from their gold discoveries, most prospectors earned at most only an adequate living from their mining. Nevertheless, the gold rush gave California a worldwide reputation as the land of opportunity. The lure of wealth from gold, combined with the state's fine climate, fertile soil, and many natural resources, made California appear a promised land to generations of people who wished to build better lives.

The colorful and adventurous spirit of the gold rush still marks California with a legacy of enterprise and prosperity. California's rich agricultural production and thriving industrial commerce upholds this legacy. Nearly 150 years after the discovery of the first tiny flakes of precious yellow metal, the vivid effect of the gold rush is still recalled in the popular public reference to California as the Golden State.

1 A Glint in the Gravel

Legends of gold in California can be traced back centuries before the great gold rush of 1849. In the sixteenth century the Spanish explorer Hernando Cortés embarked on an expedition to con-

Hernando Cortés, Spanish explorer and conqueror of Mexico. He wanted to find the legendary city of gold, El Dorado.

quer and claim Mexico for Spain. While on a sea voyage near the coast of Mexico, Cortés reported sighting what he believed to be the fabled golden city of Cibola and sent a party of soldiers to explore the region. Although the patrol returned to report that they had failed to find the city of gold, the legends persisted.

Other early Spanish explorers such as Cabeza de Vaca and Sebastián Vizcaíno sent dispatches to the king of Spain reporting rumors of rich veins of gold in the New World's interior regions of California. During their conquests of the Aztecs of Mexico and the Incas of Peru, Spanish invaders did find and seize vast fortunes from gold mines worked by these civilizations and had hopes of acquiring even richer treasures in California. Although California remained under Spanish rule more than two hundred years, the Spaniards failed to find gold mines in that territory.

Dream of an Empire

In 1821 Mexico, including the province of California, won its independence from Spain. Under Mexican rule, California remained primarily an isolated region populated by native tribes, Mexican ranchers

An Ironic Memory

In an interview recorded in Richard Dillon's Fool's Gold, *John Sutter ironically recalls:*

"Strange it was, to be sure, that the Indians had never brought a piece of gold to me although they very often delivered other things which they found in the ravines. I always requested them to bring curiosities from the mountains to the fort and I recompensed [paid] them for their efforts. I received all kinds of animals, birds, plants, young trees, wild fowl, pipe clay, stones, red ochre [iron ore], etc., but never a particle of gold."

called Californios, and a few American and European settlers who had been given land grants by the Mexican government. Among the immigrants hoping to settle in California in the early years of independence was a German-born Swiss merchant named John Augustus Sutter.

Sutter had left his wife and children and fled Germany to escape creditors in 1834, eventually arriving in California in 1839, hoping to make a new life. After becoming a Mexican citizen, Sutter applied for and received from the Mexican government a land grant of nearly fifty thousand acres in the Sacramento Valley. Sutter's grant included a fertile area of land where the Sacramento and American Rivers flowed together. On this site Sutter constructed a stockade and fort, which he named New Helvetia after the ancient name of Switzerland. The garrison soon developed into a busy center of commerce that became better known as Sutter's Fort.

Sutter was determined to prosper in California. Employing several local natives as laborers, he ambitiously set out to improve his property by planting vineyards, fruit orchards, and wheat fields. He ordered the construction of a tannery and a distillery, in addition to his living quarters and office. Sutter's Fort soon became a prominent rest station for travelers and

Swiss merchant John Augustus Sutter arrived in California in 1839 and founded the settlement that would become known as Sutter's Fort.

immigrants hoping to settle in California. Confident of greater future success, Sutter wrote the following optimistic statement to his brother Jakob in Europe, as quoted by Joseph Henry Jackson in *Anybody's Gold*:

> My holdings are extensive. In truth I have not yet beheld them in their entirety. I named my new home New Helvetia in honor of the ancient Roman title of our fatherland. A crude stockade and fort were my first concern, since the savages [natives] were at times none too friendly. The venture improves steadily now, and Sutter's Fort may still live in history.[1]

Although Sutter hoped to lead a peaceful existence among his neighbors in California, by 1846 the settlement of American immigrants in the territory began to disturb the many Mexican ranchers already living there. The United States had annexed Texas from Mexico the year before, and the new American president, James K. Polk, had been elected on a platform that openly expressed American interest in acquiring California. Then in

A nineteenth-century lithograph depicts a bustle of activity at Sutter's Fort. As settlers drifted into California prior to the gold rush, Sutter's Fort developed into a prominent establishment.

June 1846, amid an atmosphere of rumor and growing resentment between Californios and American settlers, a party of American insurrectionists staged what became known as the Bear Flag Revolt and declared California an independent republic. This coincided with the outbreak of the Mexican-American War. Due to the U.S. victory in that war in 1848, Mexico formally granted the United States title to the territory.

The U.S. victory in the Mexican-American War resulted in the United States's formal acquisition of California and other territory.

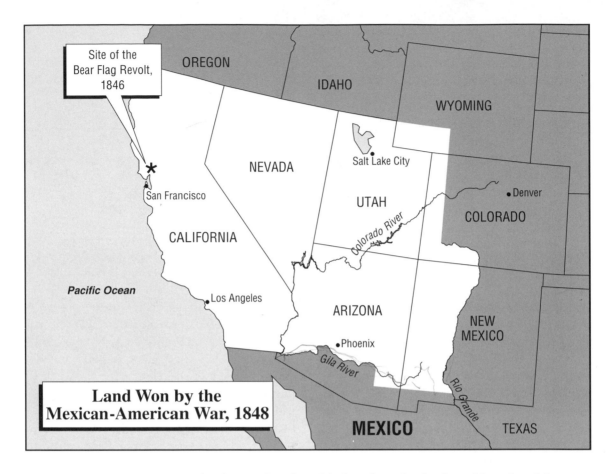

Site of the
Bear Flag Revolt,
1846

OREGON

IDAHO

WYOMING

NEVADA

Salt Lake City

UTAH

Denver

COLORADO

San Francisco

Colorado River

CALIFORNIA

Pacific Ocean

Los Angeles

ARIZONA

NEW
MEXICO

Phoenix

Gila River

Rio Grande

**Land Won by the
Mexican-American War, 1848**

MEXICO

TEXAS

During the war Sutter had remained the independent administrator of New Helvetia and continued to plan the expansion of his enterprise. By 1847 he had developed his property into a flourishing agricultural settlement. As Sutter's personal empire grew, he also developed a reputation for kindness and generosity to travelers and guests; a gracious host, he often provided them with food and clothing. In nine years Sutter had risen from impoverished immigrant to the height of his power as the administrator of a considerable domain.

Ironically, the events that would insure a place for Sutter's Fort in history would also result in the destruction of Sutter's budding empire. At the time Sutter wrote

his brother, he had no idea that his years of prosperity were nearing an end and that an unexpected incident on the American River would soon change his life forever.

To expand and develop his extensive property holdings, Sutter realized, he would need additional sources of lumber, so he hired a carpenter named James Marshall to build a sawmill for the settlement. Marshall was directed by Sutter to scout out a suitable location for the sawmill and supervise its construction. In return for his services, the two men agreed, Marshall would receive a percentage of the lumber produced at the mill.

Marshall selected a section of land on the south fork of the American River called Coloma, about fifty miles northeast of Sutter's Fort. The location seemed ideal to Sutter: it contained a stand of pine trees to furnish the lumber and an abundant supply of water to drive the mill. Approving Marshall's choice, Sutter directed his foreman to begin construction of the sawmill in the summer of 1847.

Employing a small labor force of twenty men, Marshall set to work digging a millrace, or canal, to divert water from the river to the sawmill site, where it would turn the mill wheel. To hasten the process, Marshall's crew built a series of wooden floodgates that, when opened, allowed the river water to flow into the millrace and widen the channel. As the current streamed through the millrace, it left deposits of sand and gravel in the lower end of the channel.

On Monday morning, January 24, 1848, Marshall began the day's work by inspecting the millrace to see how much the river had widened the channel during the previous night. As he walked along the muddy canal, Marshall noticed the glint of something shiny lying in the gravel. As

James Marshall's fateful discovery of gold in Coloma launched the California gold rush.

quoted by Jackson, Marshall later recalled the discovery of what he then suspected and later learned was gold:

> I went down as usual, and after shutting off the water from the race I

The Forty-Eighter

In Men to Match My Mountains *Irving Stone relates how the forty-eighters reacted differently to the discovery of gold than the forty-niners who followed.*

"The Forty-Eighter, in pursuit of gold, was a reluctant bridegroom. His portrait bears little relation to his highly publicized cousin, the Forty-Niner, yet in many ways he is the more interesting, or at least purer, personality. The early settlers had not come to California for gold, yet how could a man justify his not stooping to pick up the essence of wealth [gold] when all he had to do was scratch it out with his pocket knife?"

The canal where Marshall first noticed the shiny metal flakes that would change the course of California's history.

stepped into it, near the lower end, and there upon the rock about six inches beneath the water I discovered the gold. I picked up one or two pieces and examined them attentively. I then tried it between two rocks and found that it could be beaten into a different shape but not broken.[2]

Marshall knew that gold was a soft metal that was capable of being shaped or beaten into different shapes. He also knew that gold would not be destroyed by strong chemicals or acids. After he had gathered several more bits of the shiny metal and tied them up in a cotton rag, Marshall carried them to the camp cook, Mrs. Jenny Wimmer, who placed some of the metal into one of her wash kettles filled with lye and baking soda. To their excitement, the corrosive liquid did not change the color of the metal.

Marshall Shares His Secret

Marshall then mounted his horse and set off for Sutter's Fort to report his discovery to John Sutter. He arrived at the fort in the middle of a heavy rainstorm and hurried to his employer's office. Sutter was startled by his drenched foreman's sudden appearance. Agitated, Marshall demanded that the doors of the office be locked to insure their privacy. Sutter, aware that Marshall was considered by many as a moody and eccentric man, decided to humor his foreman and, according to historian William Weber Johnson, later recalled: "He was a singular man, and I took this to be some freak [whim] of his. I supposed, as he was queer [eccentric], that he took this queer way to tell me some secret."[3]

When the doors had been locked, Marshall withdrew from his pocket the bundle of metal flakes and showed them to Sutter. The two men tested the metal in a solution of nitric acid; again it was unchanged. They then weighed the metal on an apothecary, or druggist, scale against an equal weight of silver. Marshall's metal flakes were then submerged in water and the metal flakes sank, proving that they were a denser metal than silver. The results of these tests led Sutter to suspect that the metal Marshall had found was gold, and he made plans to visit the mill and inspect the location of Marshall's discovery as soon as the storm ended. Marshall, eager to return to the sawmill to search for more gold, rode back to Coloma immediately. When the weather cleared several days later, Sutter set out for Coloma, still troubled by a sense of foreboding.

The possibility of a gold strike greatly troubled Sutter. As a rancher, Sutter believed that owning farmland and raising crops were the best ways of acquiring wealth. He feared that the lure of gold would draw away the workers he needed and bring in outsiders who, in their greed, could destroy his land in their search for the precious metal. William Weber Johnson quotes Sutter in his book, *The Forty-Niners:*

> The curse of the thing [the gold discovery] burst upon my mind. I saw from the beginning how the end would be, and I had a melancholy ride of it to the sawmill. Of course I knew nothing of the extent of the discovery, but I was satisfied, whether it amounted to much or little, that it would greatly interfere with my plans.[4]

At the sawmill Sutter's fears were confirmed. As he walked along the millrace, he collected several more small specimens of the metal and became convinced that the area was rich in gold deposits. Gathering the work crew at Coloma together, he asked them to remain silent about the discovery and continue working at their jobs. Although the men agreed, Sutter doubted that they would keep their promise.

Because Sutter's original land grant did not extend to Coloma, he did not hold title to the area in which the gold had been discovered, now officially considered public domain. In a desperate attempt to obtain ownership of Coloma, Sutter negotiated a three-year lease of the land with the region's native inhabitants. Sutter knew that neither the former Mexican administration nor the current American provincial government recognized Native American rights to the property but felt

Sutter's Dreams Before Coloma

Sutter's dream of wealth before the gold rush involved agricultural prosperity for New Helvetia. Included in Fool's Gold *is this portion of a letter Sutter wrote to consul Thomas Larkin in 1846.*

"We have the best prospects for a good and rich harvest. I am plowing and sowing every day. Now I am sowing peas, potatoes, preparing for corn and cotton. Vegetables I will, likewise, have a great quantity. Onions at least for about $1,000. The next fall will be a powerful immigration here. It is stated from 10 to 20,000, which I hardly can believe. I think if 2 or 3,000 would come, it would be a great many. It is good when I have plenty to eat for them. Therefore, I am building a floating mill in the American [River] Fork to furnish plenty of flour."

that such a negotiation was his only hope of possibly claiming ownership to the land.

When he had completed negotiations with the Coloma tribe, Sutter sent an employee named Charles Bennett to Monterey, then the capital of California, to ask the U.S. provisional governor, Colonel Robert B. Mason, to confirm the lease. Bennett set out on his 120-mile journey carrying a buckskin sack containing six ounces of gold dust gathered at Coloma. On his way to Monterey, Bennett stopped at a general store in a settlement called Benecia and again at the coastal town of Yerba Buena, renamed San Francisco that year, and showed the gold to people who noticed his sack and inquired about its contents. Inevitably, the sight of the gold aroused excitement among the spectators,

Charles Bennett triggered public interest when he spread the news that gold had been discovered. His revelation sent fortune seekers scrambling to the goldfields.

and Sutter's secret about the discovery at Coloma was revealed.

As Sutter feared, his crewmen soon left their jobs to hunt for gold. News of the discovery spread throughout the local area of New Helvetia, and more people joined in the prospecting. Within six weeks of Marshall's discovery, nearly all of Sutter's employees, including laborers working at his fort, had deserted him for the goldfields.

Although the number of gold seekers in the Sierra foothills was increasing, knowledge of the gold strike during 1848 was primarily restricted to local inhabitants of the region. The first published announcement of the discovery appeared as an inconspicuous notice on the back page of a newspaper called the *Californian* on March 15, 1848. As quoted by Johnson, on it read in part:

> GOLD MINE FOUND—In the newly made race-way of the saw-mill recently erected by Captain Sutter, on the American fork, gold has been found in considerable quantities. One person brought thirty dollars-worth to New Helvetia, gathered there in a short time. California, no doubt, is rich in mineral wealth.[5]

An Electrifying Announcement

The notice did little to stir further public interest in the gold strike. About a month later, however, Sam Brannan, editor of a rival newspaper called the *California Star*, set out to generate some interest in the discovery. Brannan was a Mormon elder who

San Francisco in the late 1840s. The city's population surged and economy flourished as the gold rush took root.

In San Francisco, Sam Brannan's dramatic cry of "gold, gold, gold from the American River" fueled gold fever throughout the region.

had led a group of 238 Mormons from New York to settle in California. Shortly after their arrival in the territory, Brannan had founded the *California Star*, San Francisco's first newspaper. In addition, Brannan owned and operated general stores in both San Francisco and Sutter's Fort.

Brannan was convinced he could make a fortune selling merchandise from his stores to the hordes of miners he felt sure would invade the territory in a gold rush. In mid-April 1848, he returned to San Francisco from Sutter's Fort, weary but elated. Still covered with mud from prospecting, Brannan strode through the streets of San Francisco holding a quinine bottle filled with gold dust he had found and shouted in a booming voice: "Gold, gold, gold from the American River."[6]

Brannan's announcement had an electrifying effect throughout the province. The news of the gold strike spread quickly through the territory, sending hundreds of people scrambling to the Sierra foothills. By mid-June the American consul, Thomas O. Larkin, reported that the town of San Francisco, which had a population of approximately 850, was half deserted as its citizens rushed to the goldfields. As excitement over the discovery grew, sailors aboard ships that were anchored in San Francisco Bay lowered boats into the water and deserted their vessels to prospect for gold. James Marshall's discovery of a few shining metal flakes in the muddy millrace on the American River was soon reported around the world and would escalate into the California gold rush.

Chapter

2 Gold Fever

News of the gold strike at Coloma following Sam Brannan's dramatic announcement in San Francisco swiftly spread and prompted fevered public response. Settlers deserted their homes, storekeepers closed their shops, and farmers abandoned crops to join the growing swarm of people headed for the foothills of the Sacramento Valley. Historian Irving Stone quotes one gold seeker who recorded the intense excitement he had felt after another prospector showed him the gleaming contents of a pouch filled with gold dust:

A frenzy seized my soul; houses were too small for me to stay in; I was soon in the street in search of necessary outfits; piles of gold rose up before me at every step; castles of marble, dazzling the eye with their rich appliances [furnishings]; thousands of slaves bowing to my beck and call; myriads [many thousands] of fair virgins contending with each other for my love . . . were among the fancies of my favored imagination. The Rothschilds and Astors [wealthy European families] appeared

Gold miners work hard panning and sluicing rock to find the elusive gold.

The dream of striking it rich proved to be irresistible; swarms of gold seekers headed for California to make their fortune.

dred in January 1848 to approximately four thousand by midsummer. By the end of 1848 estimates increased to eight to ten thousand people. John Sutter's Swiss gardener witnessed the hysteria of gold fever that gripped New Helvetia during this time and, as quoted in Johnson's *The Forty-Niners*, wrote:

> Exciting rumors began to spread with the rapidity of a great epidemic. Everyone was infected, and, as it spread, peace and quiet vanished. To all appearances men seemed to have gone insane, or to have suddenly lost some of their five senses; they were apparently, living in a dream. Each man had to stop and ask himself: "Am I mad? Is this all real? Is what I see with my own eyes actually gold, or is it merely my imagination? Is it Chimera [illusion]? Am I delirious?[9]

"Go Not After It, but Let Others Go"

Although gold fever had begun to inflame thousands of people, not everyone in California was swept up by the excitement. Many of the Mexican Californios who owned ranches believed that the real wealth in California existed in the cattle they raised and the crops they grew. In his book, *Men to Match My Mountains*, Irving Stone relates the reactions of two prominent Californio landowners to the gold rush:

> Luis Peralta, an aging Californio gentleman who had been given a vast grant comprising the present cities of Berkeley, Oakland and Alameda, refused to

to me but poor people; in short I had a very violent attack of gold fever.[7]

As a result of the mass exodus, the San Francisco newspaper, the *Californian,* was forced to cease publication for lack of subscribers. In its final issue the *Californian* printed the following regretful note regarding the gold strike that had resulted in the newspaper's demise: "The whole country resounds with the sordid cry of gold! GOLD! GOLD!!! while the field is left half-planted, the house half-built and everything neglected but the manufacturers of shovels and pickaxes."[8]

The number of gold seekers estimated to be prospecting in the goldfields surrounding Coloma grew from a few hun-

"Astonishing Excitements"

The news of Marshall's gold discovery was relayed to Secretary of State James Buchanan on June 1, 1848, in a report from the American consul, Thomas Larkin. Larkin's dispatch is included in the prologue of The World Rushed In.

"I have to report to the State Department one of the most astonishing excitements and state of affairs now existing in this country that perhaps has ever been brought to the notice of the Government. On the American Fork of the Sacramento and Feather rivers, there has been within the present year discovered a plácer, a vast tract of land containing gold in small particles. It is now two or three weeks since the men employed in these washings have appeared in this town [San Francisco] with gold to exchange for merchandise and provisions. I presume near $20,000 of this gold has as yet been so exchanged. I have seen several pounds of this gold and consider it very pure."

be stampeded. He said: "My sons, God has given this gold to the Americans. Had he desired us to have it, He would have given it to us ere [before] now. Therefore, go not after it, but let others go. Plant your lands, and reap; these be your best gold-fields, for all must eat, while they live."

Mariano Vallejo rode up to Coloma, watched other men successfully mining gold, picked up a few flakes as a matter of scientific interest, then rode back to his home in Sonoma, never again bothering to go into the goldfields. Nor did the Californio families from San Luis Obispo south join the rush; they remained on their land and within a year, as Luis Peralta had predicted to his sons, found that their herds of cattle were richer goldfields than Coloma or Morman Island.[10]

An Empire Is Threatened

For John Sutter the spread of gold fever was an unwelcome reality that threatened the destruction of his empire. Sutter's forebodings of financial ruin at the time of Marshall's discovery soon proved accurate. Within a few months of the discovery, thousands of miners invaded his lands, trampled his fields and vineyards, and stripped him of most of his agricultural labor force. Without laborers Sutter's land fell into neglect. Unharvested, the entire wheat crop was ruined. Many of Sutter's cattle were lost when they strayed from his property through broken fences, and many were butchered by miners for food. In addition, the desertion of his workers from Sutter's Fort forced him to close down many of the settlement's industries, including the operation of his tannery, where valuable untreated hides were left to rot.

Sutter's troubles were compounded by Governor Mason's refusal to grant him the mineral rights to the land at Coloma. In a letter written on March 5, 1848, Mason had replied to Sutter's request by denying him title to Coloma, explaining that his office could not sanction the lease since the government did not recognize the right of Native Americans to sell or lease land they occupied.

In desperation Sutter at last decided to join the growing swarm of miners headed for the goldfields with the hope of making his own gold strike. Recruiting a workforce of about fifty local natives and a small group of native Hawaiians who had recently arrived in California, Sutter led his party to prospect on a sandbar, or ridge of sand, on the south fork of the American River. Misfortune continued to plague Sutter there: rival miners harassed and bullied Sutter's laborers. Hoping to avoid conflict and failing to strike gold on the American River, Sutter moved his party to another area in the southern Sierra foothills that would later become known as Sutter's Creek. Once again Sutter was disappointed in his prospecting attempts and decided to abandon mining. According to Richard Dillon in his book, *Fool's Gold*, Sutter recalled his failure in later years:

> It was high time to quit this sort of business, in which I only lost time and money. I therefore broke this camp, too, and returned to the fort where I disbanded nearly all of the people who had worked for me in the mountains digging gold. The whole expedition proved to be a heavy loss to me.[11]

The First Rich Strikes

Although Sutter's mining efforts had ended in failure, the rich strikes made by other prospectors were causing wild excitement. One of these fortunate individuals was Sutter's own former private secretary, John Bidwell. A native of New York, Bidwell had moved westward to Ohio with his parents as a boy.

As a young man Bidwell worked as a schoolteacher but soon grew restless in this occupation and eventually left his job to explore the territories of Kansas and Missouri. Bidwell had heard stories from a fur trapper who had traveled to California describing the territory as a paradise. Inspired by

John Bidwell hit upon one of the richest strikes in gold rush history. Stories like his enticed others to seek their fortunes in the goldfields.

these tales, Bidwell decided to travel farther west. In the spring of 1841 Bidwell helped organize a party of families hoping to settle in California, and they set out from Sapling Grove, Missouri. After a journey filled with hardship, Bidwell successfully led the first party of immigrants overland to California in November 1841.

Shortly after his arrival in California, Bidwell met John Sutter at New Helvetia and accepted a job as Sutter's administrative assistant. Bidwell proved to be a capable and reliable employee, and the two men became close friends. By 1847 Bidwell had saved enough money to buy his own land, which he named Rancho Chico near the Feather River. Following Marshall's fateful discovery at Coloma the next year, Bidwell visited the sawmill site and noted that the gravel in the American River was similar to that in the Feather River on his own property.

Bidwell returned to his ranch and began prospecting along the river with a few companions. On July 4, 1848, he discovered what eventually proved to be one of the richest strikes of the entire gold rush

at a location that later became known as Bidwell's Bar. Bidwell, who William Weber Johnson quotes, recorded his discovery in a brief statement that was exceptional for its composure: "Dickey Northgraves and I went to what is now Bidwell's Bar and there found gold and went to mining."[12]

Another rich strike was made by an ox-team driver named John Sullivan in the summer of 1848. Sullivan discovered a gully, later known as Sullivan's Creek, near the Stanislaus River from which he took twenty-six thousand dollars in gold dust. Reports of such fabulous claims circulated rapidly throughout the gold camps and convinced the growing number of miners that gold lay hidden in the Sierra foothills, mountains, and valleys far beyond the site of the original discovery.

A Shrewd Entrepreneur

Fortunate prospectors were not the only people growing wealthy from gold fever. True to Sam Brannan's prediction, the

The lure of gold and adventure brought prospectors pouring into California, leading to a rapid growth in the state's population.

"A Pocket Full of Rocks"

A typical example of the excited newspaper publicity given to the gold rush is this portion of an editorial written by Horace Greeley for the New York Daily Tribune *and included in* The Forty-Niners *by William Weber Johnson.*

"We are all fairly afloat. We don't see any links of probability missing in the golden chain by which Hope is drawing her thousands of disciples to the new El Dorado, where fortune lies abroad upon the surface of the earth as plentiful as the mud in our streets, and where the old saying a pocket full of rocks meets a golden realization. The perilous stuff [gold] lies loose upon the surface of the ground, or only slightly adheres to rocks and sand."

Many of the colorful stories of miners striking it rich were nothing but stories.

gold rush brought merchants and other entrepreneurs opportunities to make money off the prospectors. Following the demise of the *Californian,* Brannan closed the offices of his own *California Star* and concentrated his efforts in supplying his two stores at San Francisco and Sutter's Fort with merchandise.

Anticipating the miners' needs, Brannan had shrewdly purchased all of the iron and tin pans available in San Francisco, knowing they were essential pieces of equipment to prospectors panning for gold. Brannan bought the pans for twenty cents apiece and sold them to miners in exchange for an ounce of gold valued as high as sixteen dollars. In addition, Brannan's stores stocked clothing, food, and tools, all sold to miners at a tremendous profit.

Colonel Mason's Tea Caddy

Miners in general did not appear to mind paying such exorbitant prices. Most were confident that they would grow wealthy from their prospecting and freely spent

This engraving of San Francisco was made one year after the gold rush began. The city's rapid population growth led to a thriving economy.

any gold they found. There were few disputes over claims, and comparatively few crimes, reported during the first year of the gold strike. In a report made of a tour of the goldfields during the summer of 1848, and quoted in *The Forty-Niners*, Colonel Mason remarked:

> I was surprised to learn that crime of any kind was very infrequent, and that no thefts or robberies had been committed. All live in tents, in bush houses, or in the open air, and men have frequently about their persons thousands of dollars-worth of this gold; and it was to me a matter of surprise that so peaceful and quiet a state of things should exist. Conflicting claims to particular spots of ground may cause collisions, but they will be rare, as the extent of the country is so great, and the gold so abundant, that for the present there is room and enough for all.[13]

During his inspection of the goldfields, Mason traveled first to Sutter's Fort and then up the American River to a mine, called Mormon diggings, worked by a group of Mormons. From there Mason visited the site of Marshall's discovery at Sutter's Mill and learned that one claim worked at a ravine in the region called Weber's Creek had yielded seventeen thousand dollars in gold in one week. With government funds, Mason purchased samples of gold weighed in troy units. (A troy pound weighs twelve ounces, and a troy ounce weighs 480 grains.) Mason bought gold weighing 230 ounces; 15 pennyweights, or 24 grains; and 9 grains to be delivered to Washington, D.C., along with his report. The gold was carefully packed in a tea caddy, a chest for storing a tea service, and entrusted to Lieutenant Lucien Loeser for delivery to President James K. Polk.

The gold samples delivered by Lieutenant Loeser were then sent to the mint in Philadelphia, and assayed, or valued, to be worth thirty-nine hundred dollars. An enthusiastic President Polk, criticized by many for his ardent support of western expansion, included the following statement in his opening message to Congress on December 5, 1848, as quoted in Johnson's *The Forty-Niners*: "The accounts of the abundance of gold in that territory [California] are of such an extraordinary character as would scarcely command belief were they not corroborated [confirmed] by authentic reports."[14]

The gold samples carried to Washington in Colonel Mason's tea caddy were put on display in the War Department. The gleaming collection of nuggets, flakes, and gold dust on view in the capital helped make the tall tales of gold discovery in California credible to the nation. On the day following President Polk's address to Congress, an article appeared in

By 1848, gold fever gripped the entire nation. Even President James Polk commented on the abundance of gold in California in an address to Congress that year.

Gold Fever Crosses the Ocean

By the end of 1848 news of the gold discovery reached Europe. Among the Europeans who joined the gold rush was a young Belgian named Jean-Nicolas Perlot. Perlot's recollection of Marshall's discovery is included in Gold Seeker.

"Some months before, in a distant and almost unknown country of North America, called California, a certain Captain Sutter, while digging a canal to bring water to his mill (for this captain was a miller), had found gold in abundance. He had immediately informed the government of the United States, which had recently annexed this territory following a war with Mexico, and the news had spread with astonishing rapidity. Therefore, in the course of the season, the banks of the Sacramento River had been overrun by an innumerably large crowd of miners rushing from Mexico, the United States, Peru, and Chile."

As stories of gold strikes circulated throughout the nation, California's goldfields were dubbed "El Dorado" after the fabled land of gold.

the Hartford, Connecticut, *Courant* under the headline "The Gold Fever."

The Call of El Dorado

In this article the *Courant* used the Spanish expression "El Dorado" to describe California's goldfields. El Dorado, meaning "the Golden Place," was to become a popular term used by miners during the gold rush. El Dorado was the name of the legendary Land of Gold that for centuries Spanish explorers hunted for. The *Courant*'s conclusions, quoted by William Weber Johnson, would soon prove prophetic:

The California gold fever is approaching its crisis. We are told that the new region that has just become a part of our possessions, is El Dorado after all. Thither [there] is now settling a tide that will not cease its flow until either untold wealth is amassed, or extended beggary is secured. By a sudden and accidental discovery, the ground is represented to be one vast gold mine. Gold is picked up in pure lumps, twenty-four carats fine. In a moment, as it were, a desert country, that never deserved much notice from the world, has become the centre of universal attraction.[15]

Chapter

3 The Odyssey of the Argonauts

The details of Colonel Mason's report of the California gold strike were published in newspapers around the world, resulting in an international epidemic of gold fever. Thousands of people eagerly prepared to make the long journey to California from England, Ireland, Germany, Chile, China, and elsewhere. Indeed, foreign immigration significantly increased the number of people rushing frantically to California: Of the approximately eighty-five thousand people who swarmed to the goldfields in 1849 alone, an estimated twenty-three thousand were not U.S. citizens.

Despite the worldwide response, the gold rush was particularly important to Americans. At the time of Marshall's discovery, the United States was struggling to recover from the severe economic depression that followed the 1846–1848 war with Mexico. Although the United States had acquired vast new territories, including Texas and California, at war's end the conflict had seriously depleted the national treasury. Government officials were hopeful that rich deposits of gold from California would help replenish these funds.

Gold fever in the United States drove people throughout the nation to sell their homes, farms, and businesses, borrow money, pawn their possessions, or pool their life savings to finance their journeys

As the quest for gold grew frantic, people from around the world traveled to California. These immigrants endure the long voyage from Europe to San Francisco.

(Left) The frantic search for instant wealth prompted the creation of cartoons like this one, portraying "the dream of a prospecting miner." (Below) Perhaps the most colorful figure of the gold rush is that of the forty-niner who took to the goldfields in 1849.

to the California goldfields. Particularly susceptible were bank tellers, store clerks, farmers, merchants, blacksmiths, cobblers, and other tradespeople who had earned but modest incomes all their lives.

The possibility of sudden wealth seemed to many of these people to be a fabulous dream and a great adventure. A young New York trader named William Downie later recalled how the prospect of seeking his fortune in California proved to be an irresistible lure as quoted in *The Forty-Niners*:

> Some of the tales were fabulous, and the reports of treasures found were enough to entice any man of grit and daring to challenge fortune. Many, even, who had neither quality, ventured upon the search for gold, prompted merely by the lust for gain, and the hope of escaping the yolk of poverty and the discomfort of narrow circumstances.[16]

Downie and thousands of other people set out for California in 1849. Though gold seekers continued to swarm to California for the next six years, the gold rush

was at its most intense that year, and those who made the journey to the goldfields in 1849 would become known in folklore and history as the forty-niners.

For them California appeared to be the land of promise. Many of the gold seekers made elaborate preparations for the journey. They purchased colorful outfits of red or blue flannel shirts, canvas pants, broadbrimmed hats, and high boots, convinced that such costumes were the customary clothing of prospectors. In addition to shovels, pans, and other tools for gold mining, many hopeful forty-niners purchased numerous weapons, including rifles, pistols, derringers, and daggers with which they planned, if necessary, to defend their claims.

Most of the gold seekers setting out for California believed that they were embarking on a romantic adventure, and their quest led others to bestow on them a second nickname, Argonauts. This term came from a Greek myth that tells the story of a legendary hero named Jason, who led a crew of men known as Argonauts to a distant, mysterious island in search of a fabled treasure called the Golden Fleece. The province of California seemed to many of the forty-niners to be as mythical a place as the island to which Jason sailed.

Most of the gold seekers had never been to California and had little or no idea

THE

EMIGRANTS' GUIDE,

TO

OREGON AND CALIFORNIA,

CONTAINING SCENES AND INCIDENTS OF A PARTY OF OREGON EMIGRANTS;

A DESCRIPTION OF OREGON;

SCENES AND INCIDENTS OF A PARTY OF CALIFORNIA EMIGRANTS;

AND

A DESCRIPTION OF CALIFORNIA;

WITH

A DESCRIPTION OF THE DIFFERENT ROUTES TO THOSE COUNTRIES;

AND

ALL NECESSARY INFORMATION RELATIVE TO THE EQUIPMENT, SUPPLIES, AND THE METHOD OF TRAVELING.

BY LANSFORD W. HASTINGS,

Leader of the Oregon and California Emigrants of 1842.

CINCINNATI:
PUBLISHED BY GEORGE CONCLIN,
STEREOTYPED BY SHEPARD & CO.
1845.

Prospectors sought travel guides like this one to steer them in their quest for gold.

A Wondrous and Wild Dream

Miners newly arrived in the goldfields brought with them dreams of adventure and wealth that were unaffected by impervious reality. The optimism of these Argonauts is described in The Forty-Niners.

"The newcomers listened to the tales of quick and easy wealth, wide-eyed and slack-jawed. They met whiskered, dirty men returning from the mines, carrying buckskin bags and quart pickle jars packed with gold dust, men who paid for drinks with a pinch of gold (the origin of the phrase 'how much can you get up in a pinch?'). And they met still others who were returning empty-handed. These men, bitter and often sick, told all who would listen that the big talk of easy pickings for California gold was pure humbug. But no one paid much attention to them."

how to get there. Predictably, the public demanded information detailing the best routes to California, and soon several guidebooks, maps, and travel manuals were on the market for sale to the modern-day Argonauts. One of the most popular guidebooks published at this time was *The Emigrant's Guide to California,* by Joseph E. Ware. Ware was a Saint Louis newspaperman who conscientiously compiled information on how to reach California from newspaper accounts of government reports filed by Colonel Mason and Consul Larkin. In addition, Ware researched the published journals of John C. Fremont, an army officer who had led two mapping expeditions to California in the early 1840s.

The Hardships of Sea Voyages

The variety of guidebooks offered to travelers described three ways for gold seekers to reach California. The all-water route involved a seventeen-thousand-mile sea journey from the east coast of the United States around Cape Horn at the tip of South America to the Pacific coast. Such a voyage took as long as six to eight months to complete and was filled with hardship. Argonauts who wished to make the sea voyage were charged as much as one thousand dollars to board a vessel bound for California and were provided with cramped and uncomfortable quarters.

Passengers who embarked on sea voyages around Cape Horn often suffered from severe cases of seasickness and illness resulting from unhealthy diets lacking in fresh vegetables or from consuming food that had spoiled during the long journey.

In addition, the stormy weather and turbulent ocean waters of Cape Horn made the voyage a perilous undertaking.

A Harrowing Ordeal

Argonauts unwilling to undertake such a sea voyage could choose to travel to California from the east by way of a land crossing at the Isthmus of Panama, the narrow land bridge linking north and south America. This journey involved a sea voyage that began at New York City harbor, proceeded south toward Cuba, and southwest to the Isthmus of Panama. Travelers would then disembark from their vessel at

Prospectors willingly endured hazardous sea voyages to reach the land promising fabulous riches. This poster advertises passage to California's gold region.

Argonauts cross the Isthmus of Panama, the land bridge linking North and South America. Plagued by hazards in this remote jungle, travelers were lucky to complete the journey unscathed.

the settlement of Chagres. From there they would travel inland across the isthmus, first by boat on rivers, then overland with pack trains through the jungle, until they reached Panama City on the Pacific coast of the isthmus. The Argonauts would then have to wait on the coast until a vessel arrived on which they could obtain passage to California.

The difficulties of such a trip were recorded in the journal of a New York businessman named Hiram Pierce, who made the journey to California in 1849. Pierce recounted that the sea voyage to the Isthmus of Panama was pleasant and uneventful. When the Argonauts disembarked at Chagres, however, they faced a dense tropical jungle. Forced to journey through this jungle, the travelers were menaced by alligators and plagued by swarms of mosquitoes.

At night they made camp and posted a guard while the rest of the party slept under trees. Pierce recorded his experience as a sentry in the Panama jungle, remarking, "I heard wild animals howl."[17]

The Argonauts traveled for four days through the jungles before reaching Panama City. During this journey several of the party fell ill with swamp fever, and many others suffered from intense fatigue. After reaching the Pacific coast of the isthmus, Pierce and his companions found that they had to wait thirty-five days before they were able to secure passage on a vessel due to the great scarcity of ships sailing to California. During the wait several people fell ill with cholera, and two of the settlers eventually died of the disease. Several members of Pierce's company had grown restless and short tempered during their

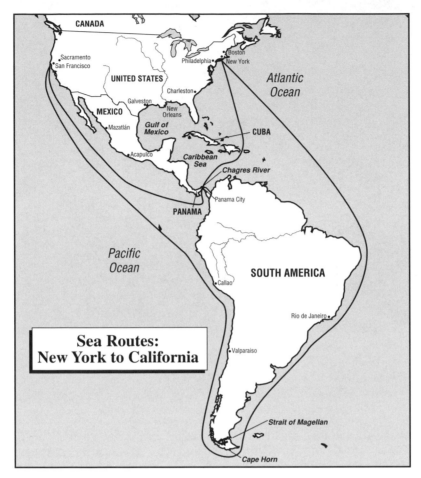

**Sea Routes:
New York to California**

enforced stay at Panama and had gotten into a fight with some natives, resulting in the stabbing death of two Argonauts.

On May 9, 1849, Pierce and his company were finally able to board a vessel bound for California and continue their journey, but the sea voyage proved no less filled with hardship. In addition to the cramped living quarters, passengers suffered from a lack of nourishing food. In his journal, quoted in Joseph Henry Jackson's book, *Anybody's Gold*, Pierce gave a depressing description of mealtime aboard ship. Pierce, like many forty-niners, was only semiliterate, and his accounts reflect this lack of formal education:

Our fare for Breakfast, coffey, hard bread and molasses. For Dinner, pork, Corned Beef & Beans or rice some times. Supper, Bread and Sugar. Butter is served, but the sight is sufficient without the Smell. Meals are taken in Hand when we can & when we cannot we go down on the deck. Our mode of living is truly brutish. For meals we form ourselves in two lines when we can, on that small part of the Deck that is clear. A man passes through with the Coffey. Another with the Sugar. Another with a basket of Bread. Another with a pan of boiled Meat. Another with a bottle of vinegar and one of Molasses & then the grabbing commences. We ketch [catch] a piece of Meat with the fingers & crowd like a lot of Swine. The ship perhaps so careened [swayed] that you will need to hold on or stagger & pitch like a Drunken man. Many behave so swineish that I prefer to stay away unless driven to it by hunger.[18]

In addition to miserable living conditions and bad food, Pierce and his fellow passengers had to endure dangerous storms at sea. In his journal, Pierce vividly recounts the terrors of such storms:

To see the fury of the Ocean, hissing, boiling and heaveing [heaving] like a Cauldron, the roar of its waters & of the tempest & the storm, the roar of the wind through the rigging & pitching of the ship combined to make a Sene [scene] truly appauling [appalling].

For my part, in the fore [earlier] part of the storm I felt [compelled] to look up to my Heavenly Father & commit to Him my Family & Soul & bid adieu to the Senes of Earth, but when I saw the ability of the Ship to ride it, I thought we should be Saved.[19]

The ship and its passengers survived the storm. Despite seasickness, bad food, and general fatigue, only one passenger died during the sea voyage, possibly resulting from eating badly cooked pork or drinking the ship's stale water. Pierce recorded the passenger's death with a somber entry in his journal:

This morning at 6 Mr. Bristol expired. Not withstanding it is the blasting of all his worldy hopes & prospects, yet in view of his sufferings it seemed a sweet releaf [relief]. His request was that his boddy might be sent home & we comenced to make preperations accordingly. So a committy [committee] was appointed to make the necessary preperations, & at 6 p.m. he was brought to the waist of the Ship, sewed

The interior of a steamer bound for California illustrates the miserable conditions endured by passengers eager to reach California at any cost.

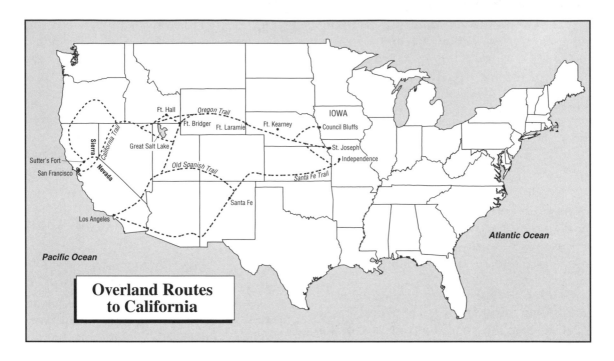

Overland Routes to California

up in canvas with his face exposed, while the English Service was gone through in a Solom [solemn] manner, after which all was sewed up & he was commited to the deep.[20]

Bristol's death was the last tragedy suffered by these travelers on their journey to California. Ten days after the burial at sea, the ship carrying the Argonauts approached San Francisco harbor. On July 26, 1849, Pierce and his companions disembarked ship, eager to begin their prospecting.

Overland to California

The third way to reach the goldfields was to travel directly overland to California. The most widely traveled overland route involved a journey that began in the vicin-

ity of Council Bluffs, Iowa, and proceeded across the Great Salt Lake Desert of Utah and finally across the Sierra Nevada into California. Such a journey was extremely hazardous. Immigrants faced possible attack from hostile Native American tribes and a brutal trek across a barren desert during which many people perished from thirst.

Another challenge that faced overland parties was the ordeal of crossing the Sierra Nevada into California. One of the primary disadvantages of traveling overland was the necessity of being able to cross this steep range before snowstorms and blizzards closed the mountain passes during the winter months. An overland journey to California took approximately eight to nine months to complete, and experienced guides advised travelers to begin their journeys in early spring in order to avoid being overtaken by winter in the mountains.

The tragic consequences that could result from failure to heed this advice had been confirmed by the fate of a caravan known as the Donner Party in 1846. Led by George Donner, who had been elected captain of the company, the settlers set out for California from Springfield, Illinois, in early summer 1846, hoping to acquire land for farming. Upon their arrival at Fort Bridger, Wyoming, the party encountered Joseph Walker, an experienced frontiersman and guide. Walker believed that the Donner Party had begun their journey too late in the year and warned against attempting to cross the Sierra Nevada so close to winter.

Disregarding Walker's advice, the party continued on into the Sierra Nevada

Overland travelers braved many perils on their journeys to California. The trek across the steep Sierra Nevada into California was particularly brutal.

The journey to California was fraught with danger, and many would-be miners never reached their goal.

and were trapped there by snow. Nearly half of the eighty-seven members of the party starved to death during their ordeal, and many of the survivors were forced to live off the flesh of their dead companions. A small party of men from the caravan, led by James Reed, finally managed to reach Sutter's Fort and return with a rescue party.

An Epic Overland Trek

Despite the fate of the Donner Party and the many dangers to be faced on the overland journey, nearly twenty-three thousand people were estimated to have made this trek to California in 1849. One of the most memorable accounts of a successful overland journey was recorded in the diary of Sarah Eleanor Royce who, with her husband, Josiah, and infant daughter, Mary, joined a caravan of covered wagons and set out for California from Council Bluffs, Iowa, in late spring 1849.

Mrs. Royce wrote vivid descriptions of life on the trail and the many adventures, hardships, and hazards the travelers faced. Many years after the trip to California, Mrs. Royce's son, Josiah, asked his mother to write down a narrative of her family odyssey to the goldfields. Mrs. Royce complied with her son's request and, referring to the original diary she kept during the trip, wrote a book titled *A Frontier Lady*. Mrs. Royce began her book with a detailed description of the commencement of their overland journey to California:

> On the last day of April, 1849 we began our journey to California. Our out-fit consisted of a covered wagon, well loaded with provisions, and such preparations for sleeping, cooking etc., as we had been able to furnish, guided only by the light of Fremont's *Travels* [guidebook written by explorer John C. Fremont], and the suggestions, often conflicting, of the many who, like ourselves, utter strangers to camping life, were setting out for the "Golden Gate."[21]

Such caravans were filled with people who had high hopes of making their fortunes in California. As the settlers journeyed westward, they often sang songs to encourage themselves. The most popular song adopted by the forty-niners was a minstrel ballad called "Oh, Susanna!" Many lyrics were made up by the prospectors and expressed their optimism and confidence in striking it rich in the goldfields. William Weber Johnson includes this version in *The Forty-Niners*:

> Then blow, ye breezes, blow!
> We're off to Californi-o.

A Poignant Message From Home

The loneliness and distress felt by the families of prospectors who went to California is expressed in a letter written by Sabrina Swain to her husband, William, and published in The World Rushed In.

"Dear Husband, this is only the 25th of August—what a long summer. O!! how I want to see you. Sometimes I almost imagine myself with you, but alas it is only the dream of fancy. May Heaven endow us with patience and grant us a happy meeting in His own due time. I long to hear from you at journey's end, which I hope will be soon. I often think what a tedious summer you have spent, makes me shudder all you must have had to pass through. May God grant that this absence and journey may prove to be a wise lesson to us both."

Images of settlers journeying westward capture the spirit of daring and adventure that characterized the era.

There's plenty of gold
So I've been told,
On the banks of the Sacramento.[22]

In her book Mrs. Royce carefully describes the day-to-day experiences of traveling west and relates moving accounts of the hardships and dangers endured by the immigrants as they faced hostile tribes and crossed parched deserts and snowy, high mountain passes. Traveling in a caravan that she described as a "city of wagons,"[23] Mrs. Royce and her family followed a route that was known as the Mormon Trail, which ran on the north side of the Platte River from Council Bluffs, Iowa, to Fort Laramie in Wyoming. The country through which they traveled was filled with buffalo herds, which were hunted by many Great Plains tribes, including Sioux, Cheyenne, and Pawnee. Mrs. Royce relates a tense confrontation between the immigrants and a party of Indians who approached the caravan demanding payment for the right to pass through the territory:

Suddenly, numerous dark moving objects appeared upon the hills in the distance, on both sides of the road. What could they be? . . . As we drew nearer they proved to be Indians, by hundreds; and soon they had ranged themselves along on each side of the way. A group of them came forward, and at the Captain's command our company halted, while he with several others went to meet the Indians and hold a parley [conference]. It turned out that they had gathered to demand the payment of a certain sum per head for every emigrant passing through this part of the country, which they claimed as their own. The men of our company, after consultation, resolved that the demand was unreasonable! that the country we were traveling over belonged to the United States, and that these red men had no right to stop us. The Indians were then plainly informed that the company

Immigrants heading west make camp in the snowy Sierra foothills. Although the lure of gold was exciting, the trip west was arduous.

meant to proceed at once without paying a dollar. That if unmolested, they would not harm anything; but if the Indians attempted to stop them, they would open fire with all their rifles and revolvers.[24]

With this warning, the settlers brandished their weapons determined to defend themselves. Confronted by this show of force, the Indians withdrew and allowed the settlers to continue their journey.

A Mystical Experience

One of the most dramatic passages in Mrs. Royce's book describes the immigrants' desperate struggle for survival as they crossed Utah's Great Salt Lake Desert, a vast, barren plain parched by the intense heat of the sun. Despite several attempts the settlers were unable to locate any streams, water holes, or springs in the

---

Toast to a Golden, Hopeful Future

Upon their arrival at Mariposa, Jean-Nicolas Perlot celebrated with friends what he believed were promising prospects of wealth. Perlot's enthusiasm was expressed in Gold Seeker.

"'Gentlemen,' I say to my companions, 'I treat today; here are the makings of a splendid banquet; we must celebrate our arrival. We have reached the end of our voyage, we are in good health, and we are going to earn our living; we have succeeded and so justified the device inscribed on the flag of La Fortune: Audaces fortuna juvat [fortune favors the bold]; it is Latin, it seems, and it means that with audacity one can always get oneself out of trouble. Therefore, we must be joyful and show it."

desert, and their meager supply of water was soon depleted. Faced with the dire possibility of perishing of thirst, Mrs. Royce prayed that her daughter, Mary, be spared from dying in the wilderness. She later related what she recalled as a mystical experience in the desert:

> Just in the heat of noon-day we came to where the sage bushes were nearer together; and a fire, left by campers or Indians, had spread for some distance, leaving beds of ashes, and occasionally charred skeletons of bushes to make the scene more dreary. Smoke was still sluggishly curling up here and there, but no fire was visible; when suddenly just before me to my right a bright flame sprang up at the foot of a small bush, ran rapidly up to it, leaped from one little branch to another till all, for a few seconds, were ablaze together, then went out, leaving nothing but a few ashes and a little smouldering trunk. It was a small incident, easily accounted for, but to my over-wrought fancy it made more vivid the illusion of being a wanderer in a far off, old time desert, and myself witnessing a wonderful phenomenon.[25]

Mrs. Royce believed that the burning bushes she had seen were a sign from God promising deliverance from dying of thirst in the desert. Strengthened by this belief, she pressed on. Mrs. Royce records that two young men who had been sent ahead to search for water returned to the caravan with welcome news:

> The two young men had been out of sight for sometime; when, all at once we heard a shout, and saw, a few hundred yards in advance a couple of hats

thrown into the air and four hands waving triumphantly. As soon as we got near enough, we heard them call out, "Grass and water! Grass and water!" and shortly we were at the meadows. The remainder of the day was spent chiefly in rest and refreshment.[26]

"The Promised Land"

With their water supply replenished, the caravan managed to complete the desert crossing and continue on to the eastern foothills of the Sierra Nevada. The mountains were the final barrier between the immigrants and California. In her book Mrs. Royce describes an arduous climb into snowy, narrow mountain passes. Riding on a mule with her daughter, Mrs. Royce found herself grateful for its sure-footed strength:

Travelers on the frontier faced confrontations with Indians who tried to prevent them from heading west.

A Journey's Summit

For many Argonauts, crossing the Sierra Nevada presented the greatest challenge of their journey to California. Included in The World Rushed In *is this excerpt from the diary of William Swain.*

"The clouds and wintry gloom vanished from the mountain tops as the rays of a clear morning sun rested upon them, and a fine southwest breeze blew gently down from the hills and gladdened the joyful hearts of all the people in our camp. I tended carefully to the teams till the sun was one hand high, and then went to camp to breakfast. All the camp was soon ready for the ascent. The teams, full of tricks, were hitched on, and the first that left the camp was No. 4, closely followed by all the train. The passage of the Sierra Nevada was fairly commenced."

The next day we climbed the first of the two ridges at the summit. And now I realized, in earnest, the value of a thoroughly trained mountain mule. In several places the way was so steep that the head of my animal was even with my eyes as I leaned forward with Mary's chief weight on my left arm while I clung with my right hand to the pommel of the saddle, obliged for the time, to let the mule guide and drive himself. And nobly he did it, never slipping once; while the dark mule did as well with his great load.[27]

After an exhausting climb the immigrants reached the summit of the mountain pass they had followed across the Sierra range. Mrs. Royce describes a thrilling event after the many weeks of hardship she had endured. The experience was the fulfillment of the hope of all Argonauts who set out on the difficult journey to California:

That night we slept within a few yards of snow, which lay in a ravine; and water froze in our pans not very far from the fire, which, however, was rather low the last part of the night. But the morning was bright and sunny. "Hope, sprang exultant": for, that day, that blessed 19th of October, we were to cross the highest ridge, view the "promised land," and begin our descent into warmth and safety.

I had purposely hastened, that morning, to start ahead of the rest; and not far from noon, I was rewarded by coming out, in advance of all the others, on a rocky height whence I looked, down, far over constantly descending hills, to where a soft haze sent up a warm, rosy glow that seemed to me a smile of welcome; while beyond occasional faint outlines of other mountains appeared; and I knew I was looking across the Sacramento Valley.[28]

Chapter

4 The Dream of El Dorado

The great dream shared by the thousands of people who swarmed into the California goldfields from 1848 to the mid-1850s was to discover the huge and elusive rich veins of gold known as the mother lode, or principal deposit. These gold veins often lay hidden deep in high cliffs or in remote areas of the mountains. The smaller deposits of gold that could be found in river and creek beds or mined from surface gravel and dirt were often found in sediment that had been worn away by water or erosion from the larger mother lode gold veins. A prospector who found color, particles of gold, in sand or gravel would stake a claim and continue to mine the area in the hope of striking it rich by finding the source of the gold.

When the Argonauts finally reached California, they were still faced with the problem of how to reach the goldfields. The final destination in California for prospectors was a rugged region of land containing many foothills and rivers where gold had been found in abundance. The approximate boundaries of the gold country and its size are described by author Dale Robertson in his book, *Wells Fargo: The Legend:*

It has been estimated that by 1852 the gold country stretched 180 miles from

Relentless in the pursuit of the mother lode—and instant wealth—a prospector tirelessly combs the hills and valleys of the gold country.

north to south, and covered about 20,000 square miles. It included all, or parts of, Amador, Calaveras, El Dorado, Mariposa, Merced, Placer, Tuolumne, and Yuba Counties. The rich lodes were found along the

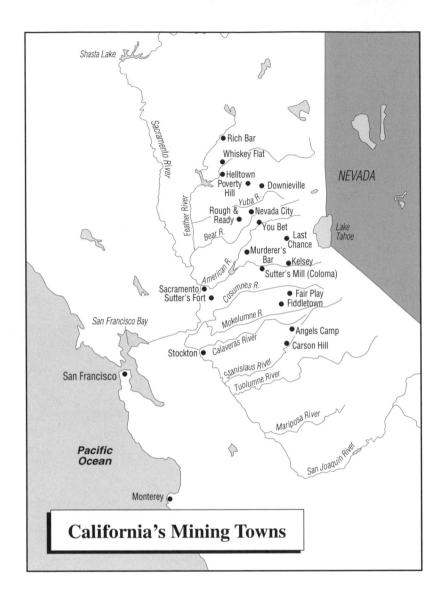

California's Mining Towns

foothills of the Sierras, and in the valleys of the American, Feather, Sacramento and the Yuba Rivers; other important amounts of gold were found along parts of the Cosumnes, Mokelumne, Calaveras, Stanislaus, Tuolumne and Merced Rivers.[29]

Upon their arrival in California exhausted gold seekers were eager to travel on to the gold rush region and endure any necessary hardships to reach the mines. Despite many difficulties, traveling overland provided immigrants a more direct route to the mines by enabling them to cross the Sierra Nevada and enter California by way of the Central Valley. Gold seekers who journeyed to California by sea arrived at San Francisco harbor, which was yet many miles away from the goldfields.

The Way to the Mines

To reach the mines from San Francisco, gold seekers had to travel inland to a juncture of the Sacramento and San Joaquin Rivers and try to obtain passage on a boat sailing up either river to Sacramento or Stockton. From there the miners could travel overland to the goldfields. Such journeys were often difficult and filled with hardship. One young miner named Enos Christman and two companions were determined to reach the gold mines and undertook the trek. Christman and his friends arrived in San Francisco in the winter of 1850 after completing a sea voyage that lasted 222 days.

Upon their arrival in San Francisco, Christman and his companions set out by boat to a settlement called San Joaquin City, located 110 miles below Stockton. Arranging for a wagon driver to carry their baggage, Christman and his friends set out on foot to the mining camp of Mariposa. Along the way they encountered a party of miners who had given up prospecting and were headed in the opposite direction. As quoted in *The Forty-Niners*, Christman recorded the encounter in his journal:

(Above) A party of prospectors journeys to the mines. (Below) An 1850 engraving of San Francisco, a thriving center during the gold rush heyday.

They told us they had been at the mines five or six months without being able to make anything, and that hundreds were working for their board [meals] alone. This did not in the least abate [decrease] our bright anticipations. We are determined to go and see for ourselves.[30]

Despite their confidence and optimism, Christman and his friends were nearly exhausted from the first day's travel. Later that evening after making camp, Christman remarked on his great weariness in his journal: "Oh, how my poor legs ache! I think I could almost rest forever."[31]

On the following day Christman and his party crossed the San Joaquin River and continued their journey eastward to the mines. After traveling on foot for five days, they crossed the Merced River and entered the foothills of the Sierra Nevada. On the following day Christman and his weary companions at last made camp among a community of miners who were busily prospecting for gold.

The living conditions that Christman found in this mining camp were similar to those encountered by many other Argonauts. Food prices had radically climbed in response to the growing demand for provisions by the increasing number of miners in the goldfields. Eggs were at a premium, ranging in price from fifty cents to three dollars apiece. Onions sold as high as two dollars each and flour for as much as eight hundred dollars a barrel.

An Exhilarating Find

Despite the high cost of living in many mining camps, most miners willingly paid the extravagant prices in the hope that a rich strike would bring them instant wealth. One of the miners who made his way to California hoping to discover a for-

An Idyllic Reminiscence

Despite the hardships of the goldfields, the description of the mining camp of Rich Bar in a letter written by Mrs. Fayette Clapp, and included in Joseph Henry Jackson's Anybody's Gold, *was anything but critical.*

"But what a lovely sight greeted our enchanted eyes as we stopped for a few moments on the summit of the hill leading into Rich Bar. Deep in the shadowy nooks of the far down valleys, like wasted jewels dropped from the radiant sky above, lay a half a dozen blue blossomed lagoons, glittering and gleaming and sparkling in the sunlight as though each tiny wavelet were formed of rifted diamonds. It was worth the whole wearisome danger, danger from Indians, grizzly bears, sleeping under stars and all to behold this beautiful vision."

Small mining communities flourished during the gold rush by selling groceries and provisions to prospectors at astronomical prices.

tune in the gold rush was a young former army officer named Edward Gould Buffum. Buffum had come to the goldfields in 1848 and wrote a vivid account of his adventures in his search for the mother lode. This excerpt of his memoirs from *The Forty-Niners* contains an enthusiastic description of his first view of the California countryside:

> The intermediate plains were dotted with autumnal flowers and open groves of evergreen oak. Herds of elk, black-tailed deer and antelope browsed near the mountain sides. Far in the distance the massive peak of Shasta reared its snow-capped head from amid a dense forest, fourteen thousand feet into the sky.[32]

Buffum and a companion arrived in the mining camp called Weaver's Creek with high hopes of making a rich strike. Two days later, while prospecting for the first time in the clay and gravel of a ravine,

Buffum made a discovery that he later recalled as an exciting and memorable event:

> I shall never forget the delight with which I struck and worked out a crevice. Getting down into the excavation I had made I commenced a careful search and at last found a crevice extending longitudinally along the rock. It appeared to be filled with a hard bluish clay and gravel, which I took out with my knife, and there at the bottom, strewn along the whole length of the rock, was bright yellow gold, in little pieces about the size and shape of a grain of barley.[33]

Buffum went on to relate his elation over the realization that he had actually found a small deposit of gold:

> Eureka! Oh how my heart beat! I sat still and looked at it some minutes before I touched it, feeling a sort of independent bravado in allowing it to

This 1875 photo shows what camp life might have been like for the Argonauts. Crude dwellings and primitive conditions were typical in most mining camps.

remain there. When my eyes were sufficiently feasted I scooped it out with the point of my knife and an iron spoon. I weighed it and found that my first day's labor in the mines had made me thirty-one dollars richer than I was in the morning.[34]

An Exception in Camp Comfort

In their quest for gold, miners like Buffum were often forced to endure primitive living conditions. Many lived in caves or under trees, while others constructed shelters such as tents or crude shacks made of poles and brush. In sunny weather such living conditions could sometimes be

pleasant. Upon reaching the goldfields, Sarah Royce and her family set up camp in the midst of a grove of pine trees. She relates in her journal an enthusiastic account of her enjoyment of this life:

With a bit of awning stretched over the least sheltered side, and a few yards of cloth tacked from one tree to another on the side toward the road, a delightful kitchen was at once improvised. Here our cook-stove was set up, our cupboard placed on a box to raise it from the ground, then fastened firmly to a tree our dining table and a few seats arranged at a little distance, and at once, we had not only kitchen, but dining room; pleasanter, for the season and situations, than indoor rooms could be.[35]

A Rugged Existence

Such pleasant living arrangements, however, were generally rare in most gold camps. Most prospectors chose to spend their time working their claims and generally devoted very little time to improving their living quarters. In rainy weather many miners suffered from frequent colds and rheumatism from sleeping in wet clothing or in the mud. In addition, miners also suffered from poor health because food in the camps was not very nutritious. Many gold seekers contented themselves with a meal of bacon, beans, and coffee. Fruits and vegetables were rare, and as a result, miners suffered from scurvy. In addition, many miners cared little for personal hygiene. Miners often failed to build adequate sanitation facilities in their camps; many seldom bothered to bathe regularly or launder their clothing.

Such difficult living conditions were widespread during the first years of the gold rush in 1848 and 1849 and often extended into many of the larger settlements located in the gold country in the Sacramento Valley. One of these settlements was the town of Sacramento, which had grown into a small community on a tract of land that John Sutter sold at public auction in 1849. Author Elisabeth Margo quotes Dr. J. D. Stillman, who wrote a description of the grim living conditions in the community of Sacramento and surrounding regions during the rainy winter of 1849:

The people at home [living away from California] can have no conception of the amount of suffering in the vicinity of this city. Hundreds are encamped in tents, through the rains and storms, scantily supplied with food and covering. Men are driven from the mines for want of food, and are begging for employment, asking only subsistence. Yesterday there were twenty-five deaths. The sickness [in general] does

Most prospectors endured grim living conditions in hopes of striking it rich. The shelter pictured in this engraving was probably comparatively better than most dwellings in the gold country.

not arise from the severity of the climate but largely from overwork, scanty and bad food, disappointment and homesickness.[36]

Fabulous Discoveries Enhance the Myths

Most of the Argonauts were willing to endure such hardships in the hope that their hard work and persistence in mining would be rewarded by acquiring fabulous wealth. Buffum's modest gold strike was similar to those experienced by thousands of other miners.

Although nearly a half-million people were drawn to the California goldfields during the six years of the gold rush between 1848 and 1854, the rich mother lode gold veins remained disappointingly elusive to most prospectors who worked hopefully at their claims with pans, shovels, and other hand tools. The few individ- uals who were fortunate enough to make a rich strike, however, acquired vast wealth, and their fabulous gold discoveries became legendary in California history.

Some of the largest strikes were made during the earliest months of the gold rush. One of the most impressive mining success stories involved two brothers, John and Daniel Murphy. The Murphys traveled overland to California and made their way to Calaveras County in 1848 with the intention of prospecting for gold. After a few days of digging, the Murphys struck pay dirt, a miner's expression meaning a rich gold discovery. By the end of 1848 the mining efforts of the Murphys had yielded them a fortune of one and a half million dollars in gold.

Another early strike that proved immensely rewarding was John Bidwell's discovery of gold on a large sandbar on the Feather River. The site of Bidwell's discovery, known as Bidwell's Bar, became one of the most famous gold mines of the gold rush. In later years Bidwell became a pros-

Another view of camp life illustrates the plight of miners who lived without the comforts of home.

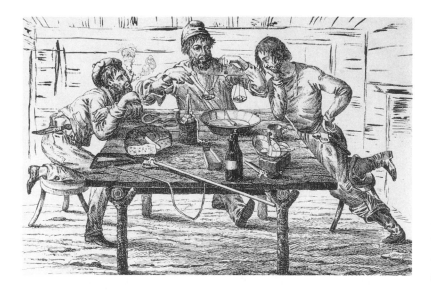

Gold miners eagerly weigh their gold particles. While most gold discoveries were modest, colorful stories of rich strikes dot the history of the gold rush.

perous rancher and founded the city of Chico, California, which grew into a prominent agricultural center.

Many miners envied the good fortune of individuals like the Murphys and John Bidwell. To former army officer John C. Fremont, the news that gold had been discovered on his own property came as a complete surprise. Fremont had won national fame as an explorer and had led the first mapping expedition across the Sierra Nevada into California while serving as an

Prospects for Matrimony

Many women living in gold camps were as eager to get married and begin families as prospectors were to strike it rich. This excerpt from a newspaper notice, included in Johnson's The Forty-Niners, *was a typical advertisement.*

"A HUSBAND WANTED

By a lady who can wash, cook, scour, sew, milk, spin, weave, hoe (can't plow), cut wood, make fires, feed the pigs, raise chickens, rock the cradle (gold rocker, I thank you Sir!), saw a plank, drive nails, etc. These are a few of the solid branches; now for the ornamental. 'Long time ago' she went as far as syntax [orderly word arrangement], read Murray's Geography and through two rules in Pike's Grammar. Could find 6 states on the Atlas, could read, and you see she can write. Can—no *could*— paint roses, butterflies, ships & c [etc.], but now she can paint houses, whitewash fences, &c."

officer in the U.S. Topographical Corps. Fremont had also been a major military leader in the American conquest of California in the war between the United States and Mexico.

In 1847 Fremont decided to retire from the army and purchase land for a ranch in northern California on which he eventually planned to live with his family. Fremont gave his business agent, former consul Thomas Larkin, three thousand dollars to buy a large section of land near the San Jose mission located south of San Francisco. Fremont was infuriated to learn that Larkin had instead mistakenly purchased forty-five thousand acres of dry land in the Sierra foothills. The error proved to be a fortunate mistake for Fremont, however, when gold was discovered on the land.

Fremont named his property the Mariposa and hired some Mexican miners to work the land, which proved fabulously rich in gold deposits. Shortly after prospecting the Mariposa, Fremont's workers sent several buckskin sacks to his home in Monterey, each containing one

John Fremont became fabulously wealthy when rich gold deposits were discovered at Mariposa.

hundred pounds of gold ore valued at twenty-five thousand dollars. The vast amounts of gold taken from Fremont's land ultimately made him a wealthy man.

Stories of fabulous discoveries of huge nuggets or other fantastic finds also circulated among the mining camps in growing number and frequency. Although many of these tales were either exaggerations or fabrications, some of the stories were true.

An account is recorded, for example, of a man who discovered two thousand dollars' worth of gold under his own doorstep. Another story relates how three Frenchmen uprooted a tree stump from the middle of a main road in Coloma and dug five thousand dollars in gold from the hole. Such claims were further enticement to the thousands of prospectors who continued to swarm into the goldfields.

One exceptional strike was made in 1850 when three German miners in search of a mother lode decided to prospect an unmined region of the upper reaches of the north fork of the Feather River. While carrying water back to their campsite one evening, one of the miners realized that the banks of the creek were filled with gold dust and larger particles of gold. The discovery led to the settlement of Rich Bar, which eventually yielded an estimated twenty-three million dollars in gold.

In addition to the legitimate accounts of rich strikes made during the gold rush, many unfounded rumors claiming the discovery of fabulous gold mines circulated in the goldfields. Such rumors often caused great excitement among miners, who rushed to the site where the large deposits of gold were reported to have been found. For most prospectors, of course, eagerness turned to disappointment, and

Fremont's mill at Mariposa, the forty-five thousand acre plot of land in the Sierra foothills.

the rumors were dispelled when back-breaking labor failed to achieve results.

The Fabled Lake of Gold

One of the most famous yarns of a supposed gold discovery involved a reported lake of gold that a miner named Thomas Stoddard claimed to have discovered in 1849. Stoddard's rumor of a gold lake began when he stumbled into a small settlement on the upper Feather River one day, physically exhausted and suffering from an arrow wound in his foot. Stoddard claimed that while prospecting with a companion in the hills, he had discovered a lake where the shore was scattered with chunks of pure gold. He claimed to have gathered several samples of the gold but said that he had become lost in the mountains and was attacked by Indians. During the skirmish,

Stoddard claimed, he was wounded and while escaping had become separated from his partner. After wandering the mountains, Stoddard finally found his way to the mining camp on the Feather River.

Stoddard's story caused a sensation in the camp. Many of the miners were eager to follow Stoddard and paid him a fee to lead them back to the area where he claimed to have discovered the lake of gold. They were prevented from doing so by severe winter weather that rendered the camp snowbound for several months. The miners were forced to wait until spring to accompany Stoddard on their search.

By May 1850 the weather had cleared sufficiently for twenty-five miners to accompany Stoddard to the mountains. Despite the company's attempts to keep the expedition a secret, news of the venture spread. By the time Stoddard began his journey, nearly a thousand prospectors had joined him in the hope of staking claims on the fabulous lake.

Stories of incredible discoveries prompted miners to work night and day in search of the mother lode.

Stoddard led his companions on a six-day search in the mountains but was unable to locate the lake. He claimed that his memory of the lake's location had grown hazy during the winter months, but the miners grew suspicious of his excuses and angry over his failure to find the lake. They accused Stoddard of swindling them and threatened to hang him if he could not lead them to the lake within twenty-four hours.

Fearful for his life, Stoddard slipped out of camp while the other miners were asleep. When the miners awoke and discovered Stoddard's disappearance, the company disbanded. The search for the lake was abandoned, and Stoddard's lake of gold became one of the most famous myths of the California gold rush.

The Adventure of a Lifetime

The quest for gold, with all of its hopes, disappointments, and whatever amounts of precious metal the land yielded, was an enterprise that many miners later recalled as one of the greatest adventures in their lives. This belief was expressed by Enos Christman, the young man who had braved the perilous sea voyage around Cape Horn to reach the California goldfields in 1850.

Christman had worked several claims in many different locations only to be disappointed to find that most of them yielded very little gold. When digging and panning for gold failed to prove rewarding, Christman and his companions attempted to construct a cradle and continue their prospecting, but this endeavor also proved disappointing.

A Venturesome Society

The citizens of the boomtowns of the gold rush were among the most robust frontier people in American history. This belief was vividly asserted by writer Remi Nadeau in the foreword to his book, Ghost Towns and Mining Camps of California.

"If you want to find the essence of American character, study the people who made the Western mining frontier. For they left the restraints of society behind them and embarked on a desperate quest against the country's toughest natural obstacles. On such a background, the American spirit was painted in caricature—at its worst, and its best."

Mining establishments were brought to life by the rugged frontier people who inhabited them.

Despite such setbacks Christman continued to work in the goldfields for three years and eventually managed to accumulate one hundred ounces of gold dust. This was not a fortune, but it was enough for Christman to return to his home in Philadelphia, settle old debts, and marry his fiancée. Although he had failed to discover the mother lode, Christman, like many other gold seekers, would cherish his adventures in the California goldfields. William Weber Johnson quotes a letter that Christman wrote to a friend. The letter was filled with nostalgia of the eventful years he spent in California and of the bride to whom he returned carrying his one hundred ounces of hard-earned gold dust:

Memory carried me back to the day that I turned my face towards a land of golden promise. What trying times were those that followed. How easy it was to walk into trouble. But the thought of the dear burthen [burden; Christman's bride] on my arm broke in upon these musings and reminded me that all was well with me. Indeed my hopes have been gratified and I have realized a fortune.[37]

5 The Harsh Life of a Miner

After arriving in the goldfields, many miners discovered that they were barely able to make a living prospecting for gold. The abundant deposits of gold that ran through the Sacramento Valley and surrounding foothills and ravines of the Sierra Nevada lay concealed in a rugged country of thick forests, rocky hillsides, steep mountains, and frigid, swiftly running rivers. Thousands of prospectors panned eagerly for gold in the cold streams or worked claims in the foothills, only to earn just a few dollars a day. For most of these miners the big strike remained an elusive phantom.

In his journal Hiram Pierce recorded the typical frustration felt by many miners after their arrival in California. After his journey across the Isthmus of Panama and up the coast, Pierce settled in a mining camp on the Tuolumne River north of the town of Stockton. After completing construction of a cabin that they hoped would shelter them from the harsh winter weather, Pierce and his companions began prospecting. Joseph Henry Jackson quotes Pierce's bleak description of his first attempts at mining:

> I made the first begining to wash gold for myself. I could work but a few minutes at a time, on account of rain. A cold frosty morning & the ground was frozen hard. The Sun does not shine on our house until 9 & then so far South that his rays are feeble, & it again disappears at ½ past 3 behind the Mountain. We made an attempt at washing but with verry poor success. I had the dum [dumb] Ague [fever]. Prospects not verry bright.

A prospector pans for gold in a California stream. The work was long, grueling, and often fruitless.

Living in remote, primitive camps, miners battled many hardships, including illness and loneliness.

A bright morning but clouded up & was cold. At 1 I was attacked by a severed Ague fit. My feet & legs are much subject to cramps. Took a stiff dose of pills & feel rather down.

Worked until 12, then had a chill, followed as usual by fever. Got $4.[38]

Prospecting proved to be a dismal series of physical hardships and fruitless labors for Pierce and his companions. Pierce's journal reflects his disappointment:

Ten months since I left home & have not made a dollar but am in debt for my board & my Health seems insufficient for the task. . . . Oh the loneliness of this desolate region! No Meeting, no Society, nought but drinking & hunting on the Sabbath. At noon I had a slight chill and severe headache. In the afternoon I felt sore & stiff.[39]

After working several more weeks at various locations in the vain hope of making a rich strike, Pierce gave up the at-

tempt and decided to return to his home in New York. In the spring of 1850 Pierce boarded a ship and once again faced the ordeals of a sea journey that included a strenuous passage through the Isthmus of Panama. Pierce's journal closed with a final entry written on January 8, 1852, which recorded a happy reunion with his family: "Still weak & feeble with Chagres Fever [tropical illness named after the Panamanian river of Chagres]. Joined my family with rejoicing."[40]

Struggles Against Illness and Loneliness

Pierce's struggle against illness and loneliness was a plight shared by many other miners who chose to remain in the goldfields. The harsh and unsanitary living conditions in the camps often caused miners to fall victim to diseases such as tuberculosis, typhoid, smallpox, and cholera.

Medical treatment for prospectors was often primitive and expensive.

Miners who fell ill were often forced to seek treatment from people who claimed to have medical knowledge but in reality lacked the education necessary to treat patients. Many people claiming to be doctors conducted a thriving business giving medical advice and selling tonics and pills to miners. Prospectors were charged as much as an ounce of gold for a consultation and a dollar for a drop of medicine. Many of these medicines were merely mixtures of alcohol, water, sugar, or other flavorings and often provided no benefits to the patient.

Along with poor food and illness, miners also suffered from boredom and loneliness. Many of the miners working in the goldfields felt isolated from the civilized world. They were lonely for their families and often grew depressed and unhappy. The hardships, disappointments, and loneliness of prospecting often discouraged miners from continuing their quest for gold and convinced many Argonauts like Pierce to abandon mining and return home.

Mining Methods

Despite the failures of Pierce and other gold seekers, thousands of other miners decided to remain in the diggings, determined to strike it rich. In their pursuit of the mother lode, prospectors developed more sophisticated methods of gold mining. Many of the first people to search for gold immediately following Marshall's discovery in 1848 were unprepared to do any ambitious prospecting. They had little or

As gold fever intensified, gold seekers improvised new mining techniques. One of the most popular methods involved using a tin pan to sift gold from river sand.

no equipment. Most of them had been content to probe for particles of gold in the riverbanks with their pocketknives. Other gold seekers improvised a method of washing a quantity of river sand in basin-shaped Indian baskets that sometimes enabled them to sift out gold particles as the soil was washed away.

Miners unable to obtain Indian baskets soon adapted the same practice by using tin pans. Panning eventually became one of the most popular forms of prospecting during the gold rush. In 1848 and 1849 the abundance of gold dust, flakes, and occasional nuggets that had washed onto gravel beds or topsoil often enabled many gold seekers to gather loose gold from the ground with little effort. This gold was known as placer gold, and the simple methods first employed by miners to gather the gold was known as placer mining.

As thousands of Argonauts continued to invade the goldfields, however, placer gold was soon depleted. The forty-niners found it necessary to develop new prospecting techniques. All of the mining methods involving the washing of sand and sediment were based on the principle that gold is about eight times heavier than an equal amount of silt. The washing process allows any gold deposits in the sand to separate from the silt and enable the miner to gather the precious metal as it settles on the bottom of the washing vessel.

One of the most popular mining methods involved the use of a device called a rocker, or cradle. The rocker was a mechanism that consisted of an oblong wooden box about three feet in length and was mounted on curved wooden rockers. Wooden bars called riffles were nailed along the cradle's open end and a piece of canvas was stretched over a wooden frame and placed at a slant inside the upper end of the cradle. A metal screen called a hopper was fitted with a handle and placed at the top of the cradle above the canvas. The miner rocked the cradle with the handle as he poured water over a shovelful of gravel and sand in the hopper. The rocking motion caused the water to wash over the gravel, which strained through the hopper and canvas screen and allowed the gold sediment to gather in the riffles below.

Another popular mining technique involved the use of the cradle (pictured), a device that strained gold sediment from gravel and sand.

Use of the cradle enabled miners to process gold-bearing soil and extract the gold particles at a faster rate than panning. In addition to the cradle, prospectors devised two other mining inventions that operated on a similar principle. One of these mechanisms was called a Long Tom. This consisted of a twelve-foot wooden trough that ended in an uptilted, perforated iron sheet called a riddle, which rested on a riffle box. Miners used the Long Tom by washing loads of gravel through the riddle, where the heavier gold particles were caught by the bars.

The second device was called a sluice. This was an improved form of the Long

The Hardship of Homesickness

The sadness of being separated from home and loved ones was one of the greatest hardships suffered by miners. This sadness was poignantly expressed in Perlot's memoirs, Gold Seeker.

"He who has never left his relatives, his village, his country, can have no idea of the sorrows of exile, whether it be voluntary or forced; one must be far from those he loves to feel how strong is the cord which ties us to them, and the farther apart we are the more we feel it. All the miners, moreover, were in that situation. In any camp, the arrival of the mail was always an event; work was suspended, everyone ran, hoping to find a letter addressed to him."

Frank Leslie's Illustrated Newspaper *published this sketch of a miner who just received bad news in a letter from home.*

Miners work the Long Tom. This device washed loads of gravel through a riddle, separating gold particles from gravel.

Tom, which consisted of a series of riffle boxes fitted together. The river current was allowed to run through the sluice in a continuous flow while the miner shoveled dirt along its side. Because of its length, the sluice could process a greater amount of gold-bearing soil than the Long Tom, but it required abundant running water, so the cradle and Long Tom were kept in use at diggings where water was scarce.

The Growing Threat of Crime

The growth and development of mining in California eventually resulted in many severe problems and disputes among miners. As the number of people rushing to the goldfields continued to grow, crime became a major problem. Incidents of claim jumping, theft, robbery, and murder occurred with increasing frequency,

along with such violent offenses as assault, stabbings, and shootings. In *The Forty-Niners* William Weber Johnson describes the alarming increase of crime and bloodshed among the miners:

Civilizing trends there surely were, but there was also a shocking—and in some places, an increasing—amount of crime and bloodshed. Most of the Forty-Niners had taken too literally the stories of quick and easy wealth in California. When it became apparent that fortune came neither quickly, easily, nor, above all, with any certainty, many men expressed their frustration in irrational behavior. The easiest way was to drown disappointment and loneliness in alcohol. Great numbers drank themselves into quarrels and incoherence and even death. Thievery, almost unknown in the diggings at the outset, increased year by year, and tempers grew shorter.[41]

Racial tension between citizens and other immigrants—such as the Mexican-Americans pictured—often resulted in violence in the goldfields.

In addition, conflicts between citizens and recent immigrants—Chinese, Germans, and emigrants from South American countries—increased the violence in the goldfields. In *Men to Match My Mountains* Irving Stone describes the growing racial tension between miners on the frontier:

> Though the English, Irish, Australians and Germans were quickly assimilated, and the Californios were liked, the Chileans and Sonorans [Mexicans] respected for their mining skills, racial antagonism began to spring up among the thousands of strangers thrown together into a political vacuum. The Indians were run out of their mountains, the Chinese and Mexicans pushed out of the better claims, the French, called Ksekydees from their [constant] question, "Qu'est-ce que se dit?" ("What did you say?") remained clannish.[42]

Americans especially resented Mexican miners whom they regarded as intruders, since California had become a part of the United States. This racial tension often erupted into acts of violence against Mexicans by Americans. During the first months of the gold rush in 1848, several incidents were reported of Mexican-American miners being evicted by other prospectors from gold camps along the American River. In another confrontation three drunken Americans reportedly hanged a Mexican who objected to the Americans' use of profanity in front of his wife.

The Legend of Joaquin Murieta

This intense hostility was vividly dramatized in the legend of the infamous bandit Joaquin Murieta. Historians continue to debate whether the outlaw actually ever existed, but stories of Murieta's alleged exploits in the goldfields have become a colorful part of California history.

According to popular legend Joaquin Murieta was a young Mexican miner whose wife was raped and brother whipped by drunken American miners who had stolen Murieta's gold claim.

Murieta swore vengeance and embarked on an outlaw career, robbing and killing American miners. Several cases of murders of Americans in the goldfields were reported in newspapers, and many of

A Miner's Sabbath

Concern for the spiritual welfare of the miner and the absence of churches in which they could attend services on the sabbath prompted an anonymous contributor to compose the following reflections, which were published in Hutchings' California Magazine *and are included in* Anybody's Gold.

"Even in the fields they may think and commune [communicate through meditation] with beloved friends at home, and with their own hearts, for rather would they go forth alone, beneath the lofty dome of earth's wide temple, and there, amid the gorgeous drapery of the universe, in imagination hover round scenes and persons, far, far away, and which are to the soul, like the soothing sounds of distant music—the bright links of memory's chain, that binds them to the past—and the scenes of the day, the affections, speak to man's better nature, and he goes forth a better man on the morrow after these communings and aspirations."

The absence of churches in mining towns caused concern among some citizens. At least one anonymous writer, however, commented on the spiritual richness of a "miner's sabbath."

these crimes were believed to have been committed by Murieta. The outlaw managed to evade all attempts to capture him, and many Mexicans who were victims of racial bigotry regarded Murieta as a hero. A skeptical public began to doubt that it was possible for one man to be responsible for all of the reported exploits. Historians speculate that many crimes may have been committed by several different men claiming to be Joaquin Murieta.

By 1853 the crimes attributed to Murieta had become so numerous that the California legislature authorized Captain Harry Love to form a company of twenty rangers to seek out and capture or kill Murieta within a period of three months. After two months of intensive search, Love and his men overtook a group of Mexicans camped in Panoche Pass in central California whom they believed were bandits led by Murieta. After killing the leader, whom Love claimed was Joaquin Murieta, the rangers cut off the bandit's head and placed it in a jar of alcohol as proof of Murieta's death. Joseph Henry Jackson quotes an account of the outlaw's death that was published in the San Francisco *Herald*:

> The famous bandit, Joaquin, whose name is associated with a hundred deeds of blood, has at last been captured. The Company of State Rangers, under the command of Harry Love, have been diligent in their search for the robber and his band ever since their organization. We apprised [informed] our readers sometime since that they had received information that Joaquin was lurking in the wilds of Tulare Valley, whither they accordingly directed their search. It is re-

ported that they have encountered the robber-chief himself at the head of his band at a place called Panoche Pass. A desperate fight ensued—the robbers, well mounted, attempted to fly, but being closely pursued by the Rangers, they kept up a running fight until Joaquin and one of his lieutenants were killed; two others were taken prisoner, and three managed to make their escape. Several of their horses fell into the hands of the rangers. The victors, finding further pursuit of the fugitives useless, cut off the head of Joaquin and placed it in spirits, to be brought to the settlements as proof that the veritable robber himself had been killed.[43]

Stories of Joaquin Murieta's exploits became so numerous and popular that many of them were eventually published in 1871 as *The Life and Adventures of Joaquin Murieta, the Celebrated California Bandit*, by a writer named John Rollin Ridge, and the legend of Murieta continued to be the theme of several additional books, plays, and motion pictures.

The Miners' Code of Justice

Eventually miners found it necessary to organize among themselves a system of government that defined and protected their rights and property. The Argonauts felt a growing concern over protecting their individual claims and insuring themselves against robbery. As a result, many mining camps held meetings to draft a series of miners' rights, which were regarded by the prospectors as inviolable laws.

A Matter of Labor and Luck

The gold camps were filled with miners who often worked individual claims in close proximity to one another. This account written by a gold miner named Joseph Pownall, and included in The Forty-Niners, *describes the unpredictable prospects of mining.*

"That there is gold here and in abundance & scattered all over the Country no one who has ever been here will deny. To get it must needs require not only very hard work but a fair proposition of good luck also, the latter I consider quite essential, for one man may sink a hole & without much trouble take out 1, 2, 3, 4 or more ounces of dust daily, while his nearest neighbor, off only a few feet, equally well-accounted with all the necessary implements & withal [besides]quite as well raised, educated & good looking must content himself as well as he can with little or next to nothing."

According to one miner, finding gold requires "not only very hard work but fair proposition of good luck also."

During these meetings, elections were held by the miners to appoint a mayor, or alcalde, and other officials to insure the enforcement of the law. Hiram Pierce attended one such meeting held at the settlement of Washington Flat. A surviving document records the drafting of miners' laws there, is quoted by Joseph Henry Jackson in *Anybody's Gold*:

At a meeting of the miners upon Washington Flat, held April 1850, Mr. H. D. Pierce was chosen Chairman and Mr. Thomas Day Secretary. The

Literally thousands of people occupied the goldfields, and over time, miners developed a set of laws to protect their rights and property. J. M. Hutchings's "The Miner's Ten Commandments" (pictured) summarized these laws.

House being called to order, the Chairman stated the object of the meeting, which was to select an Alcalde [mayor] and a Sheriff. Mr. J. P. Ward was elected by Ballot to the office of Alcalde and Mr. J. Shores to the office of Sheriff. A motion was then made and carried that three men be chosen to draw up resolutions to regulate mining operations. Mr. J. F. Thompson, P. T. Williams and Mr. Thomas Day were chosen as such committee.[44]

Miners' laws were fundamentally the same throughout gold country and applied primarily to gold mining. These laws were summarized by an English miner named J. M. Hutchings in a document he composed called "The Miner's Ten Commandments." Included in this document, as quoted by Jackson, were the following provisions:

Thou shalt have no other claim than one. Thou shalt not make unto thyself any false claim, nor any likeness to a mean man by jumping [stealing] one. Thou shalt not steal a pick or a shovel or a pan from thy fellow miner; nor take away his tools without his leave

History or Hoax?

The legend of California bandit Joaquin Murieta gained further notoriety when a large jar filled with alcohol and containing the head of a man state rangers claimed to have been Murieta was placed on public display. Suspicion over the validity of this claim was expressed in an article in the San Francisco Alta *published on August 23, 1853, and quoted in the booklet* The Return of Joaquin *by William B. Secrest.*

"It affords amusement to our citizens to read the various accounts of the capture and decapitation of the 'notorious Joaquin Murieta.' The humbug is so transparent that it is surprising any sensible person can be imposed upon by the statements of the affair which have apeared in the prints. A few weeks ago a party of native Californians and Sonorians started for the Tulare Valley for the express and avowed purpose of running mustangs. Three of the party have returned and report that they were attacked by a party of Americans, and that the balance of their party, four in number, had been killed; that Joaquin Valenzuela, one of them, was killed as he was endeavoring to escape, and that his head was cut off by his captors and held as a trophy. It is too well known that Joaquin Murrieta was not the person killed by Captain Harry Love's party at the Panoche Pass. The head recently exhibited in Stockton bears no resemblance to that individual, and this is positively asserted by those who have seen the real Murrieta and the spurious [false] head."

WILL BE
EXHIBITED
FOR ONE DAY ONLY!
AT THE STOCKTON HOUSE!
THIS DAY, AUG. 12, FROM 9 A. M., UNTIL 6, P. M.
THE HEAD
Of the renowned Bandit!
JOAQUIN!
AND THE
HAND OF THREE FINGERED JACK!
THE NOTORIOUS ROBBER AND MURDERER.

"JOAQUIN" and "THREE-FINGERED JACK" were captured by the State Rangers, under the command of Capt. Harry Love, at the Arroya Cantina, July 24th. No reasonable doubt can be entertained in regard to the identification of the head now on exhibition, as being that of the notorious robber, Joaquin Muriatta, as it has been recognised by hundreds of persons who have formerly seen him.

A poster advertises the exhibition of the head of the legendary bandit Joaquin Murieta. Some speculate that this was nothing more than a hoax.

These gallows are a grim reminder of the lawlessness— and violent punishment— that characterized the gold rush days.

[permission]; nor borrow those he cannot spare; nor return them broken.[45]

The Harsh Justice of the Gold Camps

In addition to enforcing the fundamental miners' code, many prospecting communities relied on their alcalde to judge cases involving such crimes as shootings over gambling disputes, horse stealing, common theft, and other offenses. The enforcement of law and order in the goldfields was consistent with the rugged and harsh existence of the forty-niners and expressed in many ways the average miner's philosophy of life and fair play in the diggings. Justice to the honest miner was based on a fundamental code of honor and self-reliance and was upheld with swift and sometimes violent punishment.

Convicted thieves were sometimes branded or had their ears cut off. Whippings were administered as a common form of punishment for many misdemeanor offenses, and convicted felons were often hanged. The severity of such punishments, however, served to effec-tively curtail crime in many prospecting communities. Historian John Walton Caughey reports one vivid example of miners' justice, as recorded by a prospector named Richard J. Oglesby:

> I was present, one afternoon . . . and saw with painful satisfaction, as I now remember, Charley Williams whack three of our fellow citizens over the bare back, twenty-one to forty strokes, for stealing a neighbor's money. The multitude of disinterested spectators had conducted the court. I think I never saw justice administered with so little loss of time or at less expense.[46]

The forty-niners' first attempts at self-government stemmed from an elementary desire to insure fairness and order in prospecting and gold mining. Although the rules they devised and enforced were in many ways primitive, they were also often very effective in diminishing crime in regions of the country that were lawless and dangerous. Though frontier laws were often harsh and severe, their basic principles of justice laid a foundation of social order that would eventually serve as a basis of state government for California.

6 Boomtowns, Ballads, and Bandits

Boomtowns offered miners much needed relief from the lonely hardships of prospecting in the wilderness. Boomtowns sprang up throughout the goldfields of the Sierra valleys and foothills. The forty-niners gave many of them colorful and often eccentric names, including Shirt-Tail, Bloody Run, Whiskey Slide, Chicken Thief Flat, Dirty Bar, and Chucklehead Diggings. Others were named for the founder of the settlement, such as Jackson, named for Colonel Alden Jackson, or in honor of the miners' native lands such as Sonora, a Mexican state.

The Flourishing Boomtowns

As mining communities grew in the goldfields, prospectors were no longer restricted to a grueling routine of laboring at their claims, cooking primitive meals over campfires, and sleeping outdoors or in tents. Many boomtowns opened restaurants that offered miners a variety of meals that were a welcome change from a steady diet of bacon, beans, and coffee.

Examples of the kind of food served to miners in boomtown restaurants are

As fortune seekers scrambled to California, boomtowns developed to meet the needs of the growing population.

Nestled between the wooded mountains is Downieville, the site of one of the first major boomtowns to develop in the gold rush years.

recorded in a menu preserved from the El Dorado Hotel in the mining town of Placerville and reprinted in *Anybody's Gold*. The menu lists the following meals and prices:

> Mexican [beef], prime cut, $1.50; Mexican, up along, $1; Plain, with one potato, fair size, $1.25; Baked Beans, plain, $.75; baked beans, greased, $1; two potatoes, medium size, $.50. Hash, low grade, $.75; Hash, 18 carats, $1. Codfish balls, per pair, $.75; Grizzly roast, $1; Jackass rabbit, whole $1.[47]

One of the first major boomtowns to appear in the goldfields was Downieville, named for Major William Downie. In December 1849 Downie discovered a rich gold deposit at the juncture of the Yuba River and its north fork, located in the Sierra foothills. The discovery led to the rapid growth of Downieville, which Downie later described, as quoted by William Weber Johnson: "People began to build small houses, cabins or shanties. Men began to organize matters; to build only in certain positions, and to leave space for future streets."[48]

As boomtowns flourished, merchants realized that they could do a thriving business by contracting teamsters to haul supplies and tools by wagon or mule caravans to the goldfields and the merchandise to miners. Several merchants opened general stores in boomtowns, which enabled prospectors to purchase equipment and provisions without having to leave their claims and travel to larger settlements like Sacramento or San Francisco.

Rowdy Miners

Saloons and gambling halls also began flourishing in these towns. They often attracted rowdy crowds of miners. Prospectors seeking relief from the hard labor and tedium of working their claims frequently became intoxicated and engaged in brawls or fistfights. In addition to this boisterous behavior, disputes often arose in the gambling halls over such card games as faro and poker, sometimes leading to gunfights and killings.

Miners who decided to leave their claims and go to town generally went well armed with Colt revolvers and hunting knives. The rugged and often violent life in the California gold mines and boom-towns required that the forty-niner be self-reliant and prepared to defend his property or his life against the greed or hostility of others in order to survive.

Occasionally miners sent for their families to join them in boomtown settle-ments. The arrival of the prospectors' wives and children helped bring a degree of civilization to the California frontier. Churches and town halls were con-structed in many mining towns. People who had traveled thousands of miles across the country to settle in California gathered in these towns for Sunday church services and socialized with their

A Long Night's Revelry

The consumption of alcohol in the boomtowns often led to rowdy behavior. One boisterous night of drinking was described in the journal of a miner named John Dobie, included in William Weber Johnson's The Forty-Niners.

"The Store was crowded when we returned & about dark a good many were tolerable tight or in other words ½ drunk & after dark they got to singing sailor songs & playing games & c got us all up & Tom Baldwin played the fiddle for them & they danced and sung till near morning not letting us sleep any. Angiers has his wife here with him & she was greatly disturbed by the noise and obscene Language. Such is California."

Raucous behavior was common in the saloons and gambling halls that flourished in the boomtowns.

neighbors much as they had in the homes they had left behind.

Gold Rush Legends

Life on the frontier during the gold rush was marked by colorful legends and personalities. As the need for efficient communication and transportation grew, for example, several enterprising individuals began to devise means of developing effective mail delivery to the miners.

One of the most ambitious of these men was an adventurer named Alexander Todd. Realizing the demand by prospectors for a reliable mail delivery service, Todd invested his savings in a rowboat and began his own business as a letter carrier for the miners. In addition, Todd also decided to expand his postal service and provide passage for prospectors on a ferry business. In return for these services, Todd charged a fee of four dollars a letter

and a ferry charge of sixteen dollars a passenger. The boldness of Todd's enterprise is described in Irving Stone's *Men to Match My Mountains*:

> Determined to go to San Francisco to find the mail he was certain was there, Todd first toured the neighboring camps and registered at a dollar a head those miners who wanted him to bring back their mail. At Stockton the merchants asked Todd if he would also carry their gold to San Francisco; when he agreed they put $150,000 of dust into a butter bag! He charged the merchants five percent of the gold he carried.[49]

As Todd's business began to show profit, several other men followed his example and began mail delivery services of their own. Their postal routes often took them on long treks beyond the goldfields and over the high, snowy ranges of the Sierra Nevada. Mail carriers would stop at

A Night on the Town in Mariposa

In Gold Seeker *Perlot relates how, upon his arrival at the mining camp of Mariposa, he proceeded to seek out friends for an evening's entertainment.*

"Mariposa was on the way to becoming a city. There were already many brick houses; all the commerce of the region was concentrated there. Having arrived on Friday evening, I planned to leave again on Saturday morning; but some shipboard companions, whom I found there, decided that I would stay until Monday morning; most of them being occupied, they did not have the leisure to see me on another day. I invited them to dinner at Chanac's [a restaurant] in order to have an hour of fun together once again."

various mining camps and towns along their routes and deliver the mail to other outposts or to wagons and pack trains to be carried to other settlements.

The journeys undertaken by the mail carriers were often filled with hazards and hardships. Mail carriers sometimes faced dangers from Indian attacks or risked freezing to death in snow-covered mountain passes. Tales of perilous treks and the adventures of men who endured them became a part of California folklore. One of the most famous letter carriers, earning a reputation for courage and extraordinary stamina, was a man known as Snowshoe Thompson, who traveled on skis to deliver mail over the Sierra Nevada into Nevada.

The Overland Mail Stage

The determination and courage shown by the early mail carriers in their enterprises led to the development of more effective organized postal and public transportation systems in California. As new roads were built in the goldfields, wagons, mule trains, and pack trains were able to expand delivery of freight, supplies, and mail to a widening area of settlements and towns.

In 1856 the growing demand in California for better transportation and communication services led Congress to pass a bill allocating funds for the formation of an overland mail stage service running from the East Coast across the United States to California. The overland mail contract was awarded to a wealthy financier named John Butterfield, who had made a fortune operating a stage line in New York.

Butterfield was a robust and colorful man with great professional drive. In *The*

Transportation pioneer John Butterfield established an overland mail stage service using Concord stagecoaches. Known for their comfort and efficiency, Concord stagecoaches moved mail, freight, and people across the country.

Westerners author Dee Brown relates a vivid description of Butterfield as a dashing and vigorous individual:

> Dressed in high leather boots, a yellow linen duster [long coat], and a flat-crowned "wide awake" hat, he seemed to be everywhere at once. He cut such a dashing figure that general stores in all the towns along the route began displaying "Butterfield" coats, hats, boots, shirts and cravats [neckties].[50]

Butterfield ambitiously proceeded to organize an efficient stage line operation that included the purchase of several well-built and swift stagecoaches known as Concords. The Concord stagecoaches, named after the city of Concord, New Hampshire, in which they were built, proved to be durable vehicles with strong suspension systems that held up well

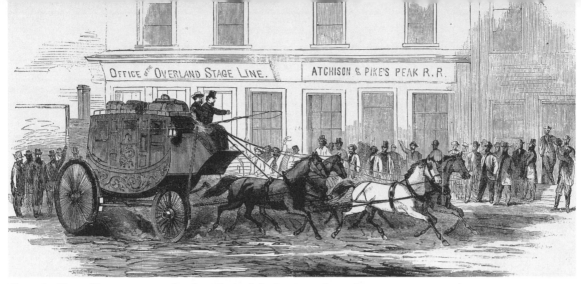

From Atchison, Kansas, an overland mail coach begins its arduous journey west.

against the rough roads and mountain trails of California. Butterfield soon expanded from mail and freight to passenger service. His efficient stage service, marked by the comfort and elegance of the Concord stagecoaches, made Butterfield's company a great success.

In 1860 Butterfield sold his overland stage service to two of his business partners, Henry Wells and William Fargo, who had formed their own express company, Wells Fargo. Historians regard John Butterfield, Henry Wells, and William Fargo as major pioneers in the development of transportation and mail service in California. The overland stage services developed by these men and the cross-country routes traveled by the Concord stagecoaches

Henry Wells (left) and William Fargo (right) created a huge stagecoach network when they founded their own express company, Wells Fargo.

eventually led to the construction of America's first transcontinental railroad. The firm of Wells Fargo has become one of the most successful express and banking companies in the United States.

Eager Audiences of Gold Seekers

As communication and transportation improved in California, mining began to attract a greater number of women. Many were the wives of miners who wished to join their husbands in the goldfields as they worked their claims, but the goldfields also drew women who pursued careers as singers, dancers, and entertainers. These women were often enthusiastically received by miners hungry for entertainment after working long and hard hours at their claims.

Most entertainers had to perform under primitive conditions in the gold camps. They sang and danced in crude tents that were used as theaters or danced on roughly constructed outdoor platforms that served as stages. Despite the difficulties, many entertainers considered performing in the gold camps to be an exciting and profitable way to make a living. Prospectors would often show their approval of the shows by applauding and tossing gold coins or nuggets onto the stages and at the feet of the performers.

The Exotic Lola Montez

Among the most noteworthy gold camp entertainers were Lola Montez and Lotta Crabtree.

Although wildly popular overseas and on the east coast, the exotic dancer Lola Montez received a weak reception from miners in the gold camps.

Lola Montez was born in Limerick, Ireland, in 1818. She led a stormy personal life. Montez was married three times and had several additional romances, including a highly publicized relationship with a European aristocrat named Ludwig of Bavaria that resulted in a public scandal. The publicity caused by Montez's many romances intrigued the public and increased her fame. Montez was regarded as a colorful celebrity who led an exciting and unconventional life. This reputation was further enhanced by Montez's performance of an exotic dance called the Spider Dance. In this dance Montez startled her audiences by engaging in a series of whirling motions onstage, during which

Montez's home in Grass Valley, California. In Grass Valley, Montez was well known for her eccentricity and theatricality.

several spiders made of cork, rubber, and whalebone were shaken out of her skirt.

An East Coast sensation, Montez traveled to California in 1853, where she appeared as a dancer in San Francisco and several mining camps. Despite her former popularity in Europe and New York, however, Montez was not well received by audiences in the goldfields. Prospectors were disappointed in her performances and felt that she lacked talent. In addition to the unenthusiastic response of her audiences, Montez's performances were also criticized in articles by two San Francisco newspaper editors. Montez was so angered by this criticism that she threatened to horsewhip one editor and challenged the other to a duel. Disappointed by her failure to gain popularity as a performer in California, Montez decided to retire from the stage and purchased a small house in Grass Valley, California. There, she hoped to settle down to a quiet life.

Montez soon became regarded as a local celebrity by the residents of Grass Valley. She received many visitors, who were intrigued by her fame and theatrical background. Montez's reputation for eccentricity was further enhanced when she acquired a bear cub that she kept as a pet. The bear cub became a popular attraction to visitors at her home as well as the sub-

"An Old Stager"

In The Westerners *Dee Brown records an admiring quote about John Butterfield by a newspaper reporter covering Butterfield's activities.*

"He is the most energetic president I ever saw. He appears to know every foot of the ground and to be known by everybody. Certainly if the overland mail does not succeed, it will not be for lack of his arduous exertions. He urged the men in changing horses at every station, often taking hold to help, and on one occasion driving for a short distance. He is, however, an old stager, and he is in his element in carrying on this enterprise."

ject of a humorous verse, as quoted by author Joseph Henry Jackson:

> When Lola came to feed her bear
> With confits [meats] sweet and sugar rare,
> Bruin ran out in haste to meet her,
> Seized her hand because 'twas sweeter![51]

Lola Meets Lotta

Two of the most frequent visitors to the Montez home included the owner of a nearby boardinghouse named Mrs. Mary Ann Crabtree and her six-year-old daughter, Lotta. Montez was charmed by the vivacious Lotta, and the two became close friends. Montez believed that Lotta possessed great natural gifts as a performer and began giving her lessons in singing and dancing. Lotta proved to be a gifted student and was soon performing for guests in the Montez home.

Lotta blossomed as a performer, and Montez convinced the Crabtrees that they would be able to earn a great deal of money by having their daughter perform for miners in the gold camps. One popular legend that emerged from the gold rush asserts that Montez took the little girl with her on a visit to the mining camp of Rough and Ready, where Lotta gave her first performance on top of a blacksmith's anvil while the blacksmith pounded out an accompaniment with his hammer.

Montez and Crabtree parted company in 1855, when Montez decided to revive her own singing and dancing career. After a series of disappointing career moves, Montez returned to New York, where she died in poverty in 1861.

Lotta Crabtree, however, went on to achieve a highly successful career as a performer. At the age of eight Lotta performed on the stage of a tavern in the mining camp of Rabbit Creek and received enthusiastic applause from the miners. The success of this performance encouraged the Crabtree family to tour the mines for several years, where Lotta was showered with gold coins and nuggets by miners. The Crabtrees prospered from these tours. As an adult, Lotta went on to perform in San Francisco and New York and achieved international fame as a singer and dancer. Crabtree's success as an

Under the tutelage of Lola Montez, Lotta Crabtree (pictured) achieved fame as a singer and dancer in California.

Because it attracted thousands of settlers to the area, the gold rush played a prominent role in the rapid development of San Francisco (above). (Below) San Francisco as it appears today, a thriving metropolis known throughout the world.

state of California and the people who once applauded her performances as a child, Lotta Crabtree presented a magnificent water fountain to the city of San Francisco. In *Anybody's Gold* Joseph Henry Jackson explains the personal significance of this gift:

> Lotta's Fountain, her gift to the city she loved best, still stands in San Francisco, the city that represented to her all the enchantment of the California that she had once known, the California that had given her her chance and taken her to its heart.[52]

The Rise of Two Major Cities

Both San Francisco and Sacramento matured into large, sophisticated cities during the gold rush. San Francisco, founded in 1834, was originally named Yerba Buena ("good herb" in Spanish) because of the abundance of mint plants that flourished in the region. Yerba Buena was

entertainer made her fabulously wealthy and enabled her to retire at an early age and purchase an estate in Boston, where she lived until her death in 1924.

Although Lotta chose to live the remainder of her life in the East, she never forgot her adventurous childhood in the goldfields. To express her gratitude to the a sleepy little seaport before the discovery of gold. In 1847 the population of the settlement was estimated at 459.

In 1848 San Francisco was invaded by hordes of travelers who came both by ship and overland to reach the California gold mines. The small settlement became the primary port of entry for thousands of people who poured into the territory to seek their fortunes. This tremendous surge of population dramatically expanded San Francisco as hotels, restaurants, grocery stores, general stores, laundries, saloons, and other businesses opened to meet the great demands of the forty-niners.

By 1855 the population of San Francisco had grown to fifty-five thousand. The city had grown wealthy from the great amounts of gold spent by prospectors who

had come to San Francisco either to invest their money in various real estate or business ventures or to celebrate a rich strike. By the mid-1850s it was estimated that $345 million in gold had circulated in San Francisco.

Before Marshall's discovery of gold in 1848, San Francisco was a sleepy little settlement that gave no indication of being destined for greatness. Today, it is one of the most famous cities in the world. San Francisco's internationally known nickname, the Golden Gate, derives from its prominent role during the California gold rush.

Sacramento

The property on which the site of Sacramento was established had originally been owned by John Sutter. Plagued by debts and desperate for money, Sutter had delegated his business affairs to his son. Upon hearing of his father's financial plight, John Sutter Jr. raised money to pay off some of his father's debts by selling off parcels of this property as building lots.

By early 1849 the Sacramento lots were selling at a high premium, and the population of the fledgling town had grown to twelve thousand. Although the development and growth of Sacramento never rivaled the flamboyant prosperity of San Francisco, Sacramento also played a distinctive role in California history. In 1850, two years after Marshall's discovery of gold, California was admitted to the Union. In 1854 Sacramento became the official capital for the State of California.

The gold rush spurred the development of Sacramento (pictured during its gold rush days), which became California's official state capital in 1854.

7 Riches, Wreckage, and Ruin

By 1858, the end of the first decade of the gold rush, most of the surface gold had been mined, but thousands of gold seekers continued to pour into California. An estimated six hundred million dollars in gold had been mined in California. A few of the boomtowns that had sprung up on the sites of gold discoveries had grown into permanent settlements, while many others had been deserted as the gold mines that had stimulated their growth were exhausted and abandoned. As prospectors continued to search the foothills, valleys, and riverbanks for new and richer discoveries, the quest for gold grew increasingly frantic and led to growing conflicts among the miners.

Many people, frustrated by their own failure to find a rich claim, grew envious of those individuals who had grown wealthy from fabulous gold discoveries. This jealousy often developed into heated confrontations between prospectors and wealthy mine owners. One dispute escalated into a major feud between John C. Fremont and a large group of mine operators known as the Merced Mining Company.

Although Fremont's Mariposa land-holdings had proven to be tremendously rich in gold ore, Fremont had been plagued by several lawsuits disputing the

John C. Fremont became embroiled in a major feud with the Merced Mining Company, which questioned the legitimacy of his property lines. Such disputes characterized the era.

boundary lines of his property. The court eventually ruled that Fremont's titles were legitimate and established the boundaries of his property. But the court also conceded that unrelated mining concerns were entitled to take possession of any unoccupied gold claim believed to be abandoned on the Mariposa tract. This ruling, however, did not prevent the growth of hostility between Fremont and the Merced Mining Company, which despite the court's decision, threatened to seize Fremont's mines and appropriate the gold.

In order to defend his mines against invaders, Fremont stationed a force of men in a small stone fort that he had built at his Pine Tree mine. While Fremont made preparations to strengthen the fort's defenses, members of the Merced Mining Company decided to take advantage of the court ruling that allowed miners to assume ownership of unoccupied claims. They first bribed the night watchman at another of Fremont's mines called the Black Drift and then seized the mine on the pretense that it was unoccupied. Once they had occupied the mine, they barricaded the shafts and tunnels.

Standoff at Pine Tree Mine

After seizing the Black Drift mine, the Merced Mining Company dispatched a party of sixty armed men to lay siege to the fortified Pine Tree mine. Fremont retaliated by organizing a company of thirteen men to cut off the Merced party. The confrontation resulted in a stalemate between the new occupiers of the Pine Tree mine and Fremont's men. During the standoff Fremont dispatched a messenger to alert the state governor, who responded by sending a force of militia to disband the opposing parties.

Upon the militia's arrival, Fremont proceeded to negotiate with the occupants of the mine. Several members of the Merced Mining Company, impressed by the courage that the outnumbered Fremont had shown in his willingness to defend his mine, reevaluated their alliance with the Merced Mining Company and de-

cided that the occupation of the mine had been wrong. In her memoirs, *Far West Sketches*, Fremont's wife, Jesse, later recalled how several of these invaders decided to switch loyalties to Fremont. "The better men refused to act longer with the disorder-loving faction."[53]

Mrs. Fremont records how one member of the Merced Mining Company expressed his admiration for Fremont's courage and contempt for the timidity shown by his own companions:

> "When I go gunning next time I'll make sure if we are after wild-duck or tame duck," said an Arkansas man noted and feared as a reckless leader; he came to say to the Colonel [Fremont] that as he saw they were in the wrong, he wanted to stay on the place and would do hauling of quartz [gold ore], "and help put down that Hornitas crowd [Merced Mining Company] if they stay fooling around where they've no business."[54]

The confrontation was resolved without bloodshed, and Fremont reclaimed his mines and resumed operation. The dispute that occurred on Fremont's property, which was dubbed the Mariposa War, dramatized the conflicts that developed between individual mine owners and mining organizations in their struggle for control of large gold mines. The Mariposa War was symbolic of the decline of gold mining by individual miners and the growth of mining in California as a major industry. Despite diminishing placer gold deposits, however, many individual prospectors continued their efforts to find new areas where surface gold might still be found. One method that was adopted was to build dams to divert river water to

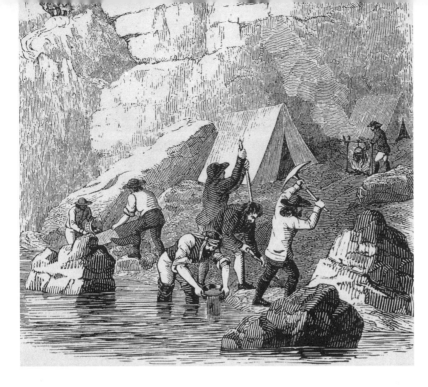

Prospectors search the riverbanks for rich deposits. As the placer gold deposits dwindled, gold diggers were forced to develop more sophisticated mining techniques.

cut new channels. Prospectors hoped that these new channels would reveal rich gold deposits in the sand and gravel over which the water flowed.

Diverting river streams involved a great deal of physical labor. But many prospectors willingly undertook the work in the hope that this new method would prove rewarding. The difficult task of damming a section of the south fork of the Feather River for gold prospecting was described in a letter written by William Swain to his brother in June 1850, as quoted in *The World Rushed In:*

> [One of the dams] was made by felling a large tree across one fork of the stream, then taking another and splitting it into planks and putting them against the tree across the river and driving them into the bottom of the river and piling stones and earth against [it] until it was tight. All the stones and earth and gravel had to be dug out of

the hills and packed in handbarrows and walked out on the tree and tipped into the river above the dam.[55]

From Placer to Quartz Mining

Diminishing placer gold deposits forced miners to combine forces to devise and finance more sophisticated methods of mining. Much of the gold ore mined was now found in deposits of quartz, a hard mineral resembling crystal, which existed in rich veins that lay deep within mountainsides or beneath the earth. One of the mining methods involved a process in which they attempted to separate the gold from quartz rock. In order to extract the embedded gold, mining companies purchased special equipment to crush the quartz rock. A large machine called a stamp pulverized the gold-bearing quartz with hammerlike blows and was powered by a single steam engine.

When the quartz had been mined and crushed, miners separated the gold from the powdered rock with methods similar to those used in placer mining, washing the gold-bearing powder in much the same way that a placer miner washed river sand in a pan. Mechanisms similar to cradles, such as sluices and riffle boards, were also used in the process.

For a brief time quartz mining grew rapidly as a major method of gold mining. Large mine owners like John C. Fremont purchased several stamps for the operation of his Mariposa gold mines and eventually extracted an estimated three million dollars in quartz gold. By 1852, 108 mills, representing an investment of almost six million dollars were in operation in the goldfields. Despite these ambitious investments, quartz mining eventually proved to be a difficult and often unprofitable method of mining. The inefficient milling processes used to separate the gold from the crushed rock resulted in the estimated loss of two-thirds to four-fifths of the gold because the stamps used to crush the gold often did not grind the rock finely enough for effective milling.

Ultimately quartz mining accounted for only a tiny fraction of the state's gold production. Even during the decade between 1850 and 1860, when quartz mining was at its height, no more than 1 percent of the gold in California was produced by this method.

A Hazardous Method of Mining

Another method requiring a great amount of physical labor was mining by

Miners built elaborate quartz mills to extract embedded gold from quartz rock. Quartz mining was inefficient and produced little gold.

tunneling into hillsides. Miners had discovered that the richest gold-bearing gravel was to be found near the solid rock, or bedrock, foundations within hillsides. In their attempts to increase mining efficiency, prospectors would sometimes consult geologists to determine which areas should be mined. Such experts were often not available in the goldfields, however, and miners frequently resorted to unusual methods to locate the gold. Many miners used such superstitious practices as wearing a small metal box called a gold magnet over the heart in the belief that it would give off a shock if gold was near. Other prospectors preferred the use of a forked tree branch called a divining rod, which they believed would reveal the location of the precious metal by twitching if gold was nearby.

Once a site had been selected for tunneling, miners dug into the hillside using picks, shovels, and drills. As the passages into the hill or mountain grew larger, prospectors installed a series of wooden supports, consisting of timber beams, in

the tunnel to prevent it from collapsing. Such a practice was known as shoring, or timbering, the mine. Miners then gathered the rock and gravel that accumulated from their tunneling and digging and hauled it out of the tunnel for processing.

Although tunneling often yielded rich returns in gold-bearing gravel, it was also one of the most dangerous methods of mining. As the number of tunnels in a hillside grew, the danger of internal collapse increased. Despite timbering the tunnels, cave-ins were common, and miners were sometimes buried alive. In addition, miners working in the tunnels generally had limited tools and grew discouraged over undertaking such hard labor with inadequate equipment. In *The California Gold Rush* Caughey relates the immense task that often confronted miners when tunneling:

> At places like Table Mountain [a gold mine], where a basaltic [dense, gray rock] crust overlay the gold-bearing gravel, burrowing seemed like the only

"The Time Is Past"

The challenges miners faced once placer deposits dwindled were described in a letter by William Swain to his brother, included in The World Rushed In.

"The fact is that gold is plenty here and the accounts received before I left home did not exaggerate the reality. Therefore I am glad that I am here. But the time is past—if it ever existed—when fortunes could be obtained for picking them up. Gold is found in the most rocky and rough places, and the streams and bars that are rich are formed of huge rocks and stones. In such places, you will see, it requires robust labor and hard tugging and lifting to separate the gold from the rock."

One particularly hazardous method of extracting gold from the land involved tunneling into hillsides (below). Inside these tunnels (left), miners collected gold-bearing rock and gravel.

way to get to the pay dirt. At other locations the overburden was not so formidable and a surface attack appeared feasible. Yet even then there might be a good deal of nonpaying topsoil to peel off, plus the upper part of the gravel, which was too poor in gold to be worth the miner's attention. Shovel, wheelbarrow, and dump cart were puny tools with which to undertake the task.[56]

The Dynamic Devastation of Hydraulics

The disappointing amounts of gold produced by quartz mining and the hazards of tunneling led mine operators to experiment with other means of extracting gold from the land in greater volume. The practice employed by placer miners of constructing dams to divert river courses was soon adapted to more ambitious mining operations.

In 1852 a French prospector named Chabot developed the simple innovation of using a hose to carry river water from a sluice to wash his diggings. The hose enabled him to direct the flow of water wherever he wished as he washed the sand and gravel in search of gold. This method was

The history of the gold rush is marked by stories of great ingenuity. A vivid example is hydraulic mining, in which inventive miners used powerful streams of water to extract gold from mountains and hills.

further improved by another miner from Connecticut, Edward E. Matteson. Matteson came up with the idea of increasing the water pressure by attaching a nozzle to his hose. The nozzle allowed him to direct a powerful stream of water against a hillside so that the gold-bearing soil would disintegrate and be washed downward to be caught in a series of sluices. Water would then flow through and cleanse sediment from gold ore.

As prospectors expanded their mining operations, they continued to improve on Matteson's invention. Mine owners soon devised a method of piping river water down from a greater height through a se-

ries of increasingly narrower hoses connected by reinforced iron rings. As the water flowed from one section of hose into the next, pressure would build, until it blasted through a strong nozzle with tremendous force. The use of this powerful water pressure developed into a mining system known as hydraulic mining, in which tremendous blasts of water gouged huge areas out of the mountains and hills. Miners then separated the gold from the soil and rock that washed down as a result of erosion, reducing the need for digging and drilling. In *The California Gold Rush* Caughey gives a vivid description of the astonishing power of hydraulic mining:

Observers spoke with awe of the majestic power of the hydraulic, which literally ate into the hillside, undermining the higher part of the bank to bring it down in an immense slide, toppling stately trees, and loosening tons of earth, which were washed forthwith into the prepared sluice.[57]

Hydraulic mining was a massive operation. It was first necessary to select a location with a water source at a height sufficient to provide enough downhill force to supply the hydraulic hoses with adequate pressure. The hydraulic hoses were then installed, and a large sluice was constructed for the soil and gravel to

Huge hydraulic hoses blast a hillside in this photo from the 1880s. The huge torrents of water caused massive damage to the land.

travel along to a large area at the foot of the hillsides, where the sediment would gather.

Despite the advantages of enabling miners to extract gold from mountains and hills in greater volume, hydraulic mining had a devastating effect on the land. The powerful streams of water caused massive erosion as hillsides collapsed from their force. This erosion often covered nearby meadows and valleys with layers of sand, loose rocks, and gravel that resulted in soil destruction and ruined farmlands. One of the most severe examples of this damage occurred along the Yuba River, where eighteen thousand acres of choice farmland were buried by as much as a hundred feet of debris. In addition, the sediment produced by hydraulic mining filled nearby streams and rivers, greatly increasing the risk of flooding.

Reforms Against Ruin

Criticism of hydraulic mining by conservationists and farmers whose land had been devastated by flood damage eventually compelled the Land Commission to investigate complaints and evaluate the damaging effects of these mining practices. In addition, property owners seeking compensation for damages inflicted on their land filed lawsuits against hydraulic mine operators. One of the most prominent cases pitted the state of California against the North Bloomingfield Mining Company

A Pioneer's Plea

Included in Rockwell D. Hunt's book, John Bidwell: Prince of Pioneers, *is an excerpt of a speech Bidwell made to the Anti-Debris Convention in 1882, pleading for the restoration of California to its former purity.*

"My mind reverts on this occasion to the time when every stream was as pure and clear as crystal. No man can measure in dollars and cents, nor with all the gold that has been taken out or that may be taken out, the value of returning these streams to their pristine [uncorrupted] purity and of clearing the rivers and the plains, and of returning them once more to their original beauty and susceptibility to cultivation. When I saw the wide ruin already begun and greater impending ruin, I could not remain at home, and so I came here to consult with you. Whatever I can do to promote the great objects of this convention to promote peace and harmony, and to bring about such results as this momentous question now demands, will be done cheerfully and to the best of my ability."

Henry Comstock and his companions hit upon a rich streak of silver in Nevada. This discovery sent prospectors scrambling to the Nevada silver mines.

in 1884. After extensive argument and controversy, the court issued a permanent injunction restraining hydraulic miners from discharging waste matter into waterways or onto another individual's property. In 1892 Congress appointed a commission to regulate hydraulic mining, which can now be carried on only under license.

A New Bonanza

As gold deposits diminished, mining operations involving quartz and hydraulic mining declined. By 1859 the tremendous excitement generated during the gold rush had faded as prospectors, discouraged over increasingly poor yields, began drifting out of the state to seek their fortunes in mining elsewhere. In the spring of 1859 three prospectors, Patrick McLaughlin, Peter O'Riley, and Henry Comstock, crossed the Sierra Nevada and entered the Great Basin in Nevada. There the partners found evidence of gold in the region. As they worked their claim, the prospectors encountered a streak of what they later described as "some troublesome blue stuff."[58] A sample of this substance carried to an assayer at Nevada City proved to be ore containing almost pure silver.

The strike discovered by Henry Comstock and his companions proved to be fabulously rich in silver and became known as the Comstock Lode. Comstock's silver discovery in 1859 marked the end of the California gold rush. News of the strike spread swiftly and soon triggered a great stampede from the California goldfields to the Nevada silver mines.

8 The Twilight of El Dorado

The great fortunes of gold mined in the Sierra Nevada foothills and valleys during the gold rush convinced people throughout the world that California was a land of opportunity and wealth. To the vast majority of people who swarmed to the goldfields in search of riches, California was the embodiment of the legendary El Dorado. In their wild pursuit of gold, miners were often driven to search for the mother lode in remote areas of California that had existed in primitive isolation for years. This frantic quest for wealth is described by William Weber Johnson in *The Forty-Niners:*

> During the half-dozen furious years following the discovery in 1848 of gold at Sutter's Mill, there seemed never to be a moment when thousands of men were not tearing at the California earth, each of them certain that the next swing of a pick would put him on a mansion on the hill. It seemed that nearly every stream and bank, every gulch and gully from Shasta in the north to Mariposa in the south had felt a prospector's pan. In 1853 alone, an estimated 100,000 Argonauts swarmed over the mountains producing $67 million worth of gold. From Downieville to Hangtown to Sonora to Angels

Camp, the lusty mine camps rocked to the clangor of gold-grubbing, of boomtown building, of the forty-niners' crude revels and their raucous and often murderous quarrels. Monotonously their conversation turned on gold and how to find it—or the consequences of having tried.[59]

End of a Wild Quest

Although gold deposits in California had proven to be enormously rich, they were not inexhaustible. Despite continued ambitious mining operations, statistics reveal a marked decline in gold production during the 1850s. The annual output of gold dropped from eighty million dollars in 1852 to approximately forty-five million by the end of the decade. In *The Forty-Niners* William Weber Johnson describes how the dwindling gold deposits in the once rich placer country in California marked the end of an era for the Argonaut:

> There was still gold in the hills, but no longer could the little man with his wash pan and his pack mule realistically expect to make his fortune digging it. From now on, sophisticated

engineering skills and heavy machinery would be required to get out the ore. And for that little man the time had come to stand up and look around to see what he had done, to take stock of his own situation—and if he was smart, to cash in his chips and move on.[60]

As the gold rush drew to a close, the mass migration to California decreased, many of the mines were deserted, and mining communities throughout the gold-fields became ghost towns. For thousands of people the end of the gold rush signaled the close of the spectacular adventure of a lifetime. Despite hardship, danger, and often disappointment, the quest for gold became the most memorable event in their lives, and the excitement of seeking their fortune in a land promising fabulous wealth was sufficient reward for making the journey to California. The nostalgic affection many miners felt for their experiences in the gold rush is described by Johnson in *The Forty-Niners:*

Dwindling gold deposits signaled the end of the gold rush. The era is commemorated in lithographs like this one, which includes caricatures of Argonauts and others who participated in the great rush for gold.

Cornerstone to Progress

As prospectors deserted the goldfields, the once bustling mining communities turned into quiet ghost towns.

Still other men, after a healthy taste of the diggings, simply packed up and went back home, for the most part looking back with fondness on California and their experience scratching for gold. They lovingly preserved their miners' garb—the cracked boots, ragged trousers, faded flannel shirts, greasy broad-brimmed hats—as mementos of the great adventure. Before setting sail for home they bought gold-headed canes for themselves and Chinese silks for their mothers, wives and sweethearts. And once home they talked with increasing nostalgia of the times, only recently past, when the challenges of each day had outweighed the disappointments. If they had not become rich, they could, at least, take satisfaction in the saying that "no coward ever set out in the gold rush and no weakling ever survived it."[61]

Many historians believe that the California gold rush was the primary stimulus for the dramatic commercial progress of California. The gold rush drew worldwide attention to California, rapidly increased its population, and accelerated its cultural and commercial development as a state.

Before Marshall's discovery at Coloma, California had attracted only a few hundred American settlers. Other than several ranches, only a few settlements like Monterey, Los Angeles, and Yerba Buena existed in California, and there were no large cities. The majority of residents consisted of Native Americans, Spanish Californians, and a few European and American settlers who generally led simple lives as ranchers, farmers, or tradespeople.

As a result of the gold rush, the population in California dramatically increased from a few thousand settlers before 1849 to 380,000 in 1860 according to a state census. In *The California Gold Rush* John Walton Caughey summarizes the impact of the gold rush on the rapid development of California as a state:

But take away the initial bonanza of gold and how much less rapid and how different would the state's rise have been? With the drowsy pastoral epoch much prolonged, with Anglo-American people and ways only gradually coming into the ascendent, the tempo and doubtless the nature of her development would have been much less spectacular. . . . Notwithstanding special advantages of resources, climate, and position, it seems certain that at least for another generation or

A Flowery Tribute to the Miner

The forty-niner is often regarded as a romantic figure in history. This description of the gold miner, which appeared in an essay in Hutchings' California Magazine *and is included in* Anybody's Gold, *presents a sentimental and somewhat idealized image.*

"The miner has been California's heart. Indefatigable in everything he has undertaken appertaining to his vocation, with money or without, he has turned the river from its ancient bed and hung it for miles together in wooden boxes upon the mountain's side, or thrown it from hill to hill in aqueducts that tremble at their own airy height; or he has pumped a river dry and taken its golden bottom out. He has leveled *down* the hills, and by the same process, leveled *up* the valleys. No obstacle so great that he did not overcome it; 'can't do it' has made no part of his vocabulary; and thus, by his perseverance and industry, were the golden millions sent rolling monthly from the mountains to the sea!"

Romantic descriptions of the adventurous forty-niner remain part of gold rush folklore.

two [California] would have languished in comparative neglect, relieved by only a leisurely upsurge of population increase and economic growth.

California's real past is infinitely more vibrant. Her pioneers erected a framework for a most imposing structure, and they did it with gold for the cornerstone.[62]

A Vigor That Made History

The robust energy displayed by the forty-niners in their quest for wealth is acknowledged by many historians as a dynamic force that changed California history. Writer Remi Nadeau concurs in Ghost Towns and Mining Camps of California.

"The rush of '49 was over. For many it was hard disappointment. Back-breaking work and an ounce of gold per day were the miner's lot in '49, with diminishing fortune in the years that followed. But by sheer force of energy the Forty-niners tore the American frontier loose from its Missouri River moorings, and sent it leaping to the Pacific; gave the West Coast a powerful momentum that has never faded; and showed a world of kings and dictators that individuals, acting on their own, could make history."

The gold rush was one of the most influential events in California history.

This 1886 photo of a frontier family captures the spirit of the adventurous pioneers who migrated to California after the gold rush.

Historians agree that the gold rush also had a significant influence on the national expansion of the United States. In *The Forty-Niners* Johnson summarizes the important role of the forty-niner in helping to expand the frontier population in the United States:

> One thing he [the forty-niner] had done, quite by accident but with dizzying speed, was to expand the physical scope of the United States so that it now embraced the entire width of the North American continent. During those half-dozen years [1848–1854] the momentum of the gold had drawn to California more than a quarter of a million people from every part of the world, in contrast with the mere 14,000 that had settled there before the discovery of gold. No doubt, with or without the discovery of gold along the Pacific, the dynamic young nation would have grown to span the continent and achieve the two-ocean destiny that Americans called manifest. But under the spell of gold the enormous change had taken place with almost magical swiftness, the population hurdling fully half the country so that the intervening high plains and mountains remained nearly empty for years after California had become settled and civilized.[63]

Rich Claims to Wealthy Industries

Historians estimate that approximately two billion dollars in gold was mined in California during the hundred years that began with the discovery of gold in 1848. Despite this high figure few miners achieved their dream of striking it rich by hitting the mother lode. Although the rich mines discovered by a few fortunate individuals contributed significantly to the state's gold production, much of the gold mined in California was produced through the efforts of the tens of thousands of people who worked modest individual claims.

Even after the rush for gold had subsided, many miners remained in California to build new lives. Here, settlers construct homes and raise livestock.

Despite disappointments over their failure to discover the mother lode, many prospectors decided to remain in California and begin new lives. Many used their gold to invest in small businesses or purchase homes and farms. Many prospectors who originally worked small claims in the goldfields remained to become employees of large mine owners as the great mining boom of the gold rush led to the growth of mining as a major industry in California.

The rapid growth in population caused by the gold rush also led to the rapid expansion of cattle raising and agriculture as important state industries. As thousands of people continued to migrate to California following the gold rush, the demand for beef and farm products helped stimulate a thriving economy, not to mention competition between ranchers and farmers. The combined gold investments of prospectors also helped to finance the development of manufacturing, shipping, and banking industries in California, which rapidly became self-sustain-

ing because of population growth and the expanding network of cities.

The growing prosperity and rapid growth of California also increased the demand for the construction of more efficient transportation routes. In order to meet these demands, railroad companies recruited large labor forces. One of the most reliable sources of this labor proved to be the thousands of Chinese immigrants who had first swarmed to California during the gold rush. Despite the decline of gold production, many Chinese chose to remain in California and begin their own businesses, including laundries and grocery stores. By mid-1852 the Chinese population was estimated to be twenty thousand.

In 1864, faced with the threat of a labor strike by his white workers, Central Pacific Railroad executive Charles Crocker hired fifty Chinese in Sacramento at twenty-six dollars a month to supplement his workforce. The Chinese proved to be reliable and industrious, and by the summer of 1865 Crocker's Chinese labor force

A Gold Seeker's Confession

In Gold Seeker *Jean-Nicolas Perlot reflects on the powerful motivating influence of gold.*

"It was gold, in fact, which in such a short time had performed this marvelous metamorphosis [transformation] which struck me with astonishment, I, a savage from the mountains come down to the plains. It was gold, that vile metal, if one wishes, but that all-powerful mover, which had here accomplished the work of civilization; religion, this time, had nothing to do with it."

had increased to two thousand. Aided by the diligent labor of the Chinese, the Central Pacific, in a joint effort with the Union Pacific Railroad, completed the construction of the first transcontinental railroad on May 10, 1869.

In his book, *The California Gold Rush*, John Walton Caughey writes that some scholars believe that the desire for instant wealth was both a negative and positive influence on the cultural and social development of California:

Still others deplore the gold rush on moral grounds. The miners, they say, were rowdy; their epoch a field day for liquor dealers, gamblers, and harlots. Standards of conduct got out of hand at the very outset, making it an uphill fight to bring them [Californians] to the level [of civilization] of the East. Speculative instincts were overstimulated, and the California spirit came to be too strongly implanted in the get-rich quick pattern.

A Chinese mining camp from the 1850s. Chinese immigrants poured into California during and after the gold rush.

(Left) Chinese laborers at work on the transcontinental railroad. (Below) This lithograph titled The Slave of Gold *is from a nineteenth-century newspaper. It illustrates some of the illicit behavior associated with life in the gold country.*

Admittedly the gold rush led Californians to hasty decisions where longer tussling with the problems might have produced a better solution. Admittedly also, California's present material success is to a large extent the result of fertile soil, climate, and position, not directly derived from its golden beginning. Nevertheless, there are tangible proofs that gold was the touchstone fundamental feature that set California in motion on the course that made her what she is today, and that her gold did things for the West at large and the Pacific basin that otherwise would not have been done for a generation or perhaps at all.[64]

Despite its negative aspects, the gold rush is regarded by most historians as one of the most dynamic and influential events in California history. The legacy of thousands of miners extends even to colorful phrases that are still in common use: "I hope it pans out"; "staking a claim"; "hitting pay dirt." One of the most famous expressions associated with the gold rush is the single word *eureka*, which appears on the state seal of California. Eureka comes from a Greek word meaning "I have found it!" This exclamation vividly captures the spirit of the forty-niner's dream of riches and as a motto acknowl-

Despite the hardships, many prospectors had fond memories of their adventures in the California goldfields.

edges the great significance of the gold rush in California history.

End of a Golden Quest

An ordinary prospector named Joseph Bruff typifies the gold rush adventure. In 1849 Bruff left his job as a government draftsman in Washington, D.C., to join the California gold rush. He wrote a vivid account of his overland journey to California and of his adventures in the goldfields. During his journey Bruff suffered such hardships as being snowbound in the Sierra Nevada and nearly dying of starvation. He survived these ordeals and finally reached the goldfields, but his attempts at mining were a failure. In 1850 Bruff gave up his dream of striking it rich in California and returned home to Washington, D.C.

Despite the difficulties and disappointments he had suffered, Bruff did not regret his adventurous journey. Like many other prospectors, Bruff was grateful for the opportunity to experience the excitement of an adventurous quest for gold. Upon his return home, Joseph Bruff closed his journal with a final entry that summarized the experience he had shared with thousands of other people during the California gold rush:

I breakfasted, and entered the cars for home, and in a little over two hours, was in the bosom of my family, after an absence of two years and three months.—

Never before did I so devoutly appreciate the heart-born ballad, "Home! Sweet home!", of my departed friend John Howard Payne [a prominent writer], and none the less that I had "seen the elephant," and emphatically realized the meaning of the ancient myth—traveling in search of

THE GOLDEN FLEECE![65]

Notes

Chapter 1: A Glint in the Gravel

1. Quoted in Joseph Henry Jackson, *Anybody's Gold*. New York: D. Appleton-Century Company, 1941, p. 3.
2. Quoted in Jackson, *Anybody's Gold*, p. 15.
3. Quoted in William Weber Johnson, *The Forty-Niners*. Alexandria, VA: Time-Life Books, 1974, p. 23.
4. Quoted in Johnson, *The Forty-Niners*, p. 26.
5. Quoted in Johnson, *The Forty-Niners*, p. 26.
6. Quoted in Johnson, *The Forty-Niners*, p. 17.

Chapter 2: Gold Fever

7. Quoted in Irving Stone, *Men to Match My Mountains*. New York: Berkley Books, 1982, p. 137.
8. Quoted in Johnson, *The Forty-Niners*, p. 32.
9. Quoted in Johnson, *The Forty-Niners*, p. 32.
10. Stone, *Men to Match My Mountains*, p. 137.
11. Quoted in Richard Dillon, *Fool's Gold*. Santa Cruz, CA: Western Tanager, 1981, p. 296.
12. Quoted in Johnson, *The Forty-Niners*, p. 210.
13. Quoted in Johnson, *The Forty-Niners*, p. 38.
14. Quoted in Johnson, *The Forty-Niners*, p. 38.
15. Quoted in Johnson, *The Forty-Niners*, p. 38.

Chapter 3: The Odyssey of the Argonauts

16. Quoted in Johnson, *The Forty-Niners*, p. 43.
17. Quoted in Jackson, *Anybody's Gold*, p. 30.
18. Quoted in Jackson, *Anybody's Gold*, p. 34.
19. Quoted in Jackson, *Anybody's Gold*, pp. 34–35.
20. Quoted in Jackson, *Anybody's Gold*, p. 35.
21. Sarah Eleanor Royce, *A Frontier Lady*. New Haven, CT: Yale University Press, 1932, p. 3.
22. Johnson, *The Forty-Niners*, p. 47.
23. Royce, *A Frontier Lady*, p. 8.
24. Royce, *A Frontier Lady*, pp. 13–15.
25. Royce: *A Frontier Lady*, p. 50.
26. Royce: *A Frontier Lady*, p. 50.
27. Royce, *A Frontier Lady*, p. 72.
28. Royce, *A Frontier Lady*, p. 72.

Chapter 4: The Dream of El Dorado

29. Dale Robertson, *Wells Fargo: The Legend*. Millbrae, CA: Celestial Arts, 1975, p. 31.
30. Quoted in Johnson, *The Forty-Niners*, p. 86.
31. Quoted in Johnson, *The Forty-Niners*, p. 86.
32. Quoted in Johnson, *The Forty-Niners*, p. 79.
33. Quoted in Johnson, *The Forty-Niners*, p. 79.
34. Quoted in Johnson, *The Forty-Niners*, p. 79.

35. Royce, *A Frontier Lady*, p. 132.

36. Quoted in Elisabeth Margo, *Taming the Forty-Niner*. New York: Rinehart, 1955, p. 18.

37. Johnson, *The Forty-Niners*, p. 227.

Chapter 5: The Harsh Life of a Miner

38. Quoted in Jackson, *Anybody's Gold*, p. 86.

39. Quoted in Jackson, *Anybody's Gold*, p. 87.

40. Quoted in Jackson, *Anybody's Gold*, p. 89.

41. Johnson, *The Forty-Niners*, pp. 141–142.

42. Stone, *Men to Match My Mountains*, pp. 162–163.

43. Quoted in Jackson, *Anybody's Gold*, p. 111.

44. Jackson, *Anybody's Gold*, pp. 90–91.

45. Jackson, *Anybody's Gold*, pp. 95–96.

46. Quoted in John Walton Caughey, *The California Gold Rush*. Berkeley: University of California Press, 1948, p. 234.

Chapter 6: Boomtowns, Ballads, and Bandits

47. Quoted in Jackson, *Anybody's Gold*, pp. 384–385.

48. Quoted in Johnson, *The Forty-Niners*, p. 114.

49. Stone, *Men to Match My Mountains*, p. 194.

50. Dee Brown, *The Westerners*. New York: Holt, Rinehart and Winston, 1974, p. 147.

51. Quoted in Jackson, *Anybody's Gold*, p. 189.

52. Jackson, *Anybody's Gold*, p. 199.

Chapter 7: Riches, Wreckage, and Ruin

53. Jesse Benton Fremont, *Far West Sketches*. Boston: D. Lothrop Company, 1890, p 79.

54. Fremont, *Far West Sketches*, p. 79.

55. Quoted in J. S. Holliday, ed., *The World Rushed In*. New York: Simon and Schuster, 1981, pp. 373–374.

56. Caughey, *The California Gold Rush*, p. 258.

57. Caughey, *The California Gold Rush*, p. 260.

58. Quoted in Caughey, *The California Gold Rush*, p. 296.

Chapter 8: The Twilight of El Dorado

59. Johnson, *The Forty-Niners*, p. 207.

60. Johnson, *The Forty-Niners*, p. 207.

61. Johnson, *The Forty-Niners*, p. 227.

62. Caughey, *The California Gold Rush*, p. xvi.

63. Johnson, *The Forty-Niners*, p. 207.

64. Caughey, *The California Gold Rush*, p. 293.

65. J. Goldsborough Bruff, *Gold Rush: The Journals, Drawings, and Other Papers of J. Goldsborough Bruff*. Edited by Georgia Willis Read and Ruth Willis. New York: Columbia University Press, 1949, p. 523.

For Further Reading

Frank L. Beals, *The Rush for Gold*. Sacramento, CA: Wheeler Publishing, 1946. Biography of California pioneer John Bidwell primarily focusing on Bidwell's activities during the settlement of California and during the gold rush.

Stephen Holt, *We Were There with the California Forty-Niners*. New York: Grosset and Dunlap, 1956. Fictional story entertainingly written about the prospecting adventures of a California family during the gold rush.

Allan Nevins, *Fremont: The West's Greatest Adventurer*, vol. 1. New York: Harper and Brothers, 1927. Volume one of a two-volume biography of explorer John C. Fremont includes an account of Fremont's mining activities in California during the gold rush.

Samuel Ward, *Sam Ward in the Gold Rush*. Edited by Howard R. Lamar. Stanford, CA: Stanford University Press, 1949. An edited volume of the memoirs of a son of a wealthy New York banker recalling his adventures during the gold rush. The book is written in a flowery style that often makes the reading tedious.

Works Consulted

Dee Brown, *The Westerners*. New York: Holt, Rinehart and Winston, 1974. Entertainingly written volume describing numerous events in the history of the American West, including the California gold rush.

J. Goldsborough Bruff, *Gold Rush: The Journals, Drawings, and Other Papers of J. Goldsborough Bruff*. Edited by Georgia Willis Read and Ruth Willis. New York: Columbia University Press, 1949. Lengthy volume containing illustrations and journal entries of gold miner J. Goldsborough Bruff. The drawings by Bruff illustrating many of his adventures are well done, and the narrative is often entertainingly descriptive.

John Walton Caughey, *The California Gold Rush*. Berkeley: University of California Press, 1948. Scholarly book about the California gold rush that offers a thoughtful perspective on the sociological impact of the gold rush on American history.

Richard Dillon, *Fool's Gold*. Santa Cruz, CA: Western Tanager, 1981. Well-written biography of California pioneer John A. Sutter that details Sutter's early life and pioneering activities in California as well as his involvement in the gold rush and tragic last years.

Jesse Benton Fremont, *Far West Sketches*. Boston: D. Lothrop Company, 1890. Short volume of memoirs written by the wife of John C. Fremont, recounting their life in the West.

Erwin G. Gudde, ed., *Sutter's Own Story: The Life of General John Augustus Sutter and the History of New Helvetia in the Sacramento Valley*. New York: G.P. Putnam's Sons, 1936. An edited volume of the memoirs of John A. Sutter, the book includes intermittent narratives by the editor, offering a historical perspective on Sutter's writings.

Bret Harte, *The Luck of Roaring Camp and Other Sketches*. Chicago: Fountain Press, 1949. Collection of selected short stories by Bret Harte.

J. S. Holliday, ed., *The World Rushed In*. New York: Simon and Schuster, 1981. An edited volume containing the journals and letters of prospector William Swain.

Rockwell D. Hunt, *John Bidwell: Prince of Pioneers*. Caldwell, ID: Caxton Printers, 1942. Admiring biography of California pioneer John Bidwell, describing Bidwell's career spanning his life as a gold miner, political figure, and noted agriculturalist.

Joseph Henry Jackson, *Anybody's Gold*. New York: D. Appleton-Century Company, 1941. Entertainingly written book about the California gold rush that includes a large section listing the sites of several former gold camps and communities and their histories.

William Weber Johnson, *The Forty-Niners*. Alexandria, VA: Time-Life Books, 1974. Well-written and richly illustrated book focusing on the California gold rush. The book contains numerous quotations from contemporary individuals involved with the gold rush.

Elisabeth Margo, *Taming The Forty-Niner*. New York: Rinehart, 1955. Lively account of the gold rush from the viewpoint of women who inhabited the gold camps and goldfields, including their impact on the gold rush.

Remi Nadeau, *Ghost Towns and Mining Camps of California*. Los Angeles: Ward Ritchie Press, 1965. Illustrated volume dealing with the mining camps of the California gold rush. Entertainingly written and contains several anecdotes describing exciting events that occurred in many of the settlements.

Jean-Nicolas Perlot, *Gold Seeker*. Edited by Howard R. Lamar. New Haven, CT: Yale University Press, 1985. Well-written memoirs of a European who traveled to California to mine during the gold rush. The book contains material that is often humorous, thoughtful, and rich in descriptive detail of the life of an Argonaut.

Dale Robertson, *Wells Fargo: The Legend*. Millbrae, CA: Celestial Arts, 1975. Slim volume dealing with the history of the Wells Fargo Company. Although informally written, the book is well-researched and descriptive.

Sarah Eleanor Royce, *A Frontier Lady*. New Haven, CT: Yale University Press, 1932. Edited memoirs of Sarah Eleanor Royce who traveled overland to California with her husband and young daughter to join the gold rush. The book offers a stirring account of the hardships and adventures of their journey to California as well as their experiences in the goldfields.

William B. Secrest, *The Return of Joaquin*. Fresno, CA: Saga West Publishing Company, 1973. Well-researched illustrated booklet that examines the legend of Joaquin Murieta.

Irving Stone, *Men to Match My Mountains*. New York: Berkley Books, 1982. Well-researched and entertainingly written book chronicling many major events and individuals in the history of the American West. The book contains several chapters relating to the California gold rush.

Stewart Edward White, *Gold!* Garden City, NY: Doubleday, Page and Company, 1913. Well-researched and colorfully written novel relating the adventures of a group of young prospectors in the California gold rush.

Index

Picture Credits

Cover photo: Stock Montage, Inc.

Archive Photos, 26, 76 (both), 94, 95, 96, 101

Archive Photos/American Stock, 30

The Bettmann Archive, 13, 35, 54, 77, 79

California State Library, 100 (top)

Corbis-Bettmann, 15 (top), 25, 31, 37, 61, 65, 75

Library of Congress, 14, 15 (bottom), 20, 22, 23, 29, 32 (top), 33, 35, 39 (bottom), 41, 43, 49, 53, 55, 68, 80 (top), 81, 82, 85, 87 (both), 91, 100 (bottom)

National Archives, 50, 97

North Wind Picture Archives, 93

Stock Montage, Inc., 47 (top)

UPI/Corbis-Bettmann, 80 (bottom)

About the Author

Tom Ito is a freelance writer who resides in Los Angeles, California. His interest in the entertainment industry led him to publish *Yesteryears* magazine, a publication profiling television and radio celebrities, which he edited and distributed in the greater Los Angeles area from 1988 to 1990. Mr. Ito has served as a literary consultant for Hanna-Barbera Productions. He is listed in *Who's Who of Asian Americans* and is the author of *Conversations with Michael Landon,* a memoir.

The Mapmaker's Daughter

Bradbury Press
New York

Collier Macmillan Canada · Toronto / Maxwell Macmillan International Publishing Group · New York

M.C. HELLDORFER

THE MAPMAKER'S DAUGHTER

ILLUSTRATED BY JONATHAN HUNT

Oxford · Singapore · Sydney

Bradbury Press
Macmillan Publishing Company
866 Third Avenue
New York, NY 10022

Collier Macmillan Canada, Inc.
1200 Eglinton Avenue East
Suite 200
Don Mills, Ontario M3C 3N1

FIRST EDITION
Printed in the United States of America
1 2 3 4 5 6 7 8 9 10

The text of this book is set in Cochin Bold.
Typography by Julie Quan and Christy Hale
Title calligraphy by John Stevens

Library of Congress Cataloging-in-Publication Data
Helldorfer, Mary-Claire.
The mapmaker's daughter / by M. C. Helldorfer.
p.   cm.
Illustrated by Jonathan Hunt.
Summary: Suchen, the daughter of a mapmaker, goes on a journey
through an enchanted land to find the king's son.
ISBN 0-02-743515-6
[1. Fairy tales.] I. Hunt, Jonathan, ill. II. Title.
PZ8.H367Map 1991 [E]—dc20 89-39330 CIP AC

A NOTE FROM THE ARTIST
The paintings for The Mapmaker's Daughter *were done on*
140 lb. hot press watercolor paper. Contours and some textural
effects were drawn in with matte black ink. The ink drawings were then
painted using traditional watercolor techniques, including wash and drybrush.
White ink and gouache were used sparingly in some of the illustrations.
The paintings were then color-separated and reproduced
using four-color process.

In memory of my grandmother,
Gertrude Bormuth Helldorfer — M.C.H.

To my parents, who sent me on my
journey,
and to Priscilla Reising, who gave me
the map — J.H.

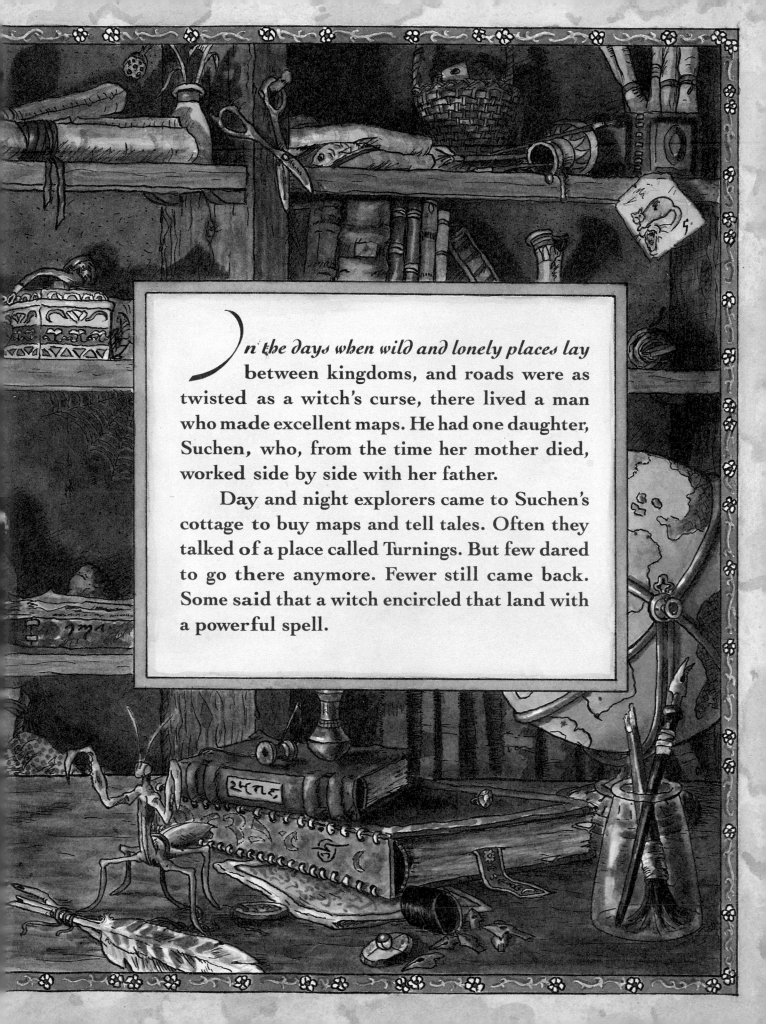

In the days when wild and lonely places lay between kingdoms, and roads were as twisted as a witch's curse, there lived a man who made excellent maps. He had one daughter, Suchen, who, from the time her mother died, worked side by side with her father.

Day and night explorers came to Suchen's cottage to buy maps and tell tales. Often they talked of a place called Turnings. But few dared to go there anymore. Fewer still came back. Some said that a witch encircled that land with a powerful spell.

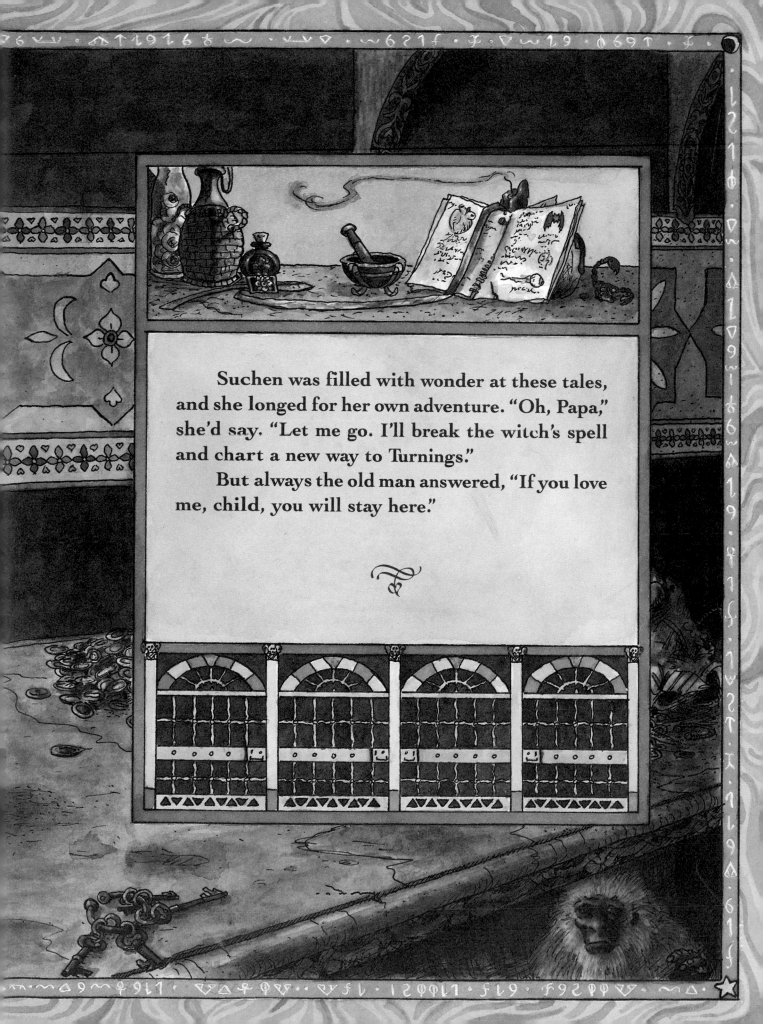

Suchen was filled with wonder at these tales, and she longed for her own adventure. "Oh, Papa," she'd say. "Let me go. I'll break the witch's spell and chart a new way to Turnings."

But always the old man answered, "If you love me, child, you will stay here."

One evening, after the mapmaker had fallen asleep, there came a soft knock at the cottage door. In rushed a man cloaked like night.

"Your Highness!" Suchen exclaimed.

"You must help me," the prince whispered. "My father wishes me safe at court. But I can sit quiet no longer."

Then he pressed a coin into Suchen's hand. "I pay you for a map to Turnings, and your trouble, too, should my father's guards come looking for me."

And Suchen fetched the map, for in the prince's eyes, she saw her own longing.

At dawn guards hammered on the mapmaker's door. The king strode in. "Arrest them both," he ordered. "My best knights are lost in Turnings. And my only son, gone on some fool's quest. I know you helped him slip away. You shall pay for his life with yours."

But Suchen pleaded, "Let me go and search for your son."

At that her father cried. The king laughed bitterly. But Suchen asked again. And, since no one else was willing to go, the king granted her wish.

Suchen hugged her father good-bye, and he gave her three gifts: her mother's white cape, a map of the way to Turnings, and a lock of his silver hair.

In the first days of adventure, the girl sang to see the paths she had once painted. But as the land grew strange, she became lonely. Sometimes she was afraid. Still, she did not stop until she reached a great river at the edge of Turnings.

A boatman waited there. "Run dry of explorers?" he asked. "All out of brave knights? Sending out princes and ladies these days?" The man shook his head. "The witch of Turnings will have room for you."

Now Suchen, hearing the word *prince*, hurried on board. But at once the boat began to sink.

"Too heavy, too heavy!" the boatman shouted, pushing the girl back on shore. "Mercy, lady, you carry too much."

"I have little," she argued, but he would not let her board again.

Then Suchen removed her mother's cape.

"Throw it into the water," the man ordered.

The girl tossed the silk. From her hand it leaped, flashed a tail, and swam away.

Suchen stared in wonder, as did the boatman. "Carrying little," he grumbled as he poled their way across the river. "Little more than a great fish."

Beyond the river, stone mountains rose before Suchen. She climbed high, and higher still, till she could climb no more.

Then a voice called down to her: "Run dry of explorers? All out of brave knights? Sending princes and ladies these days? Come, ride my goat. The witch of Turnings will have a cage for you."

And Suchen, hearing the word *prince,* eagerly climbed on the goat. All at once the animal sank beneath her.

"Too heavy, too heavy!" the goat woman cried, pushing her off. "Mercy, lady, you carry too much."

"But I have little," Suchen argued, drawing out her father's map.

"Rip it apart," the woman ordered.

Suchen tore the map in half. Out of her hands it flew: two large-winged birds.

"Carrying little," the goat woman mumbled, poking Suchen. "Two birds bigger than my goats and I!"

They wound their way through the mountains, then Suchen alighted and traveled on alone.

At last she came to the witch's castle. Every gate was watched.

"No one comes out, no one goes in unseen," she said.

"Unless they travel with me," a man replied.

"Run dry of brave knights? Sending ladies to the rescue now?" The man laughed and set a covered basket at Suchen's feet.

She climbed in quickly, then he lifted her up. But oh, how he staggered. "Lady, lady, mercy!" he cried. "You are carrying too much."

"But I have little," Suchen said, reaching into her pocket. Surely she could keep her father's lock of hair!

The man snatched it and threw it to the ground. It sprang back with a hiss and slid away.

"Carrying little," the man grunted. "Little more than a giant snake."

In darkness and silence, Suchen was carried to the heart of the castle.

Everywhere she looked — in alcoves and up the stairways, along the balconies, hanging from the great hall's ceiling — were glittering cages filled with knights and explorers and creatures strange as dreams.

Suddenly the man dropped the basket. Out Suchen tumbled. Before her stood the prince, hands and waist bound in gold.

"How nice," the witch murmured. "I like humans in twos."

Suchen scrambled back.

"What, rushing home, dear? Well, if that's your wish. Let me send you off with a little gift."

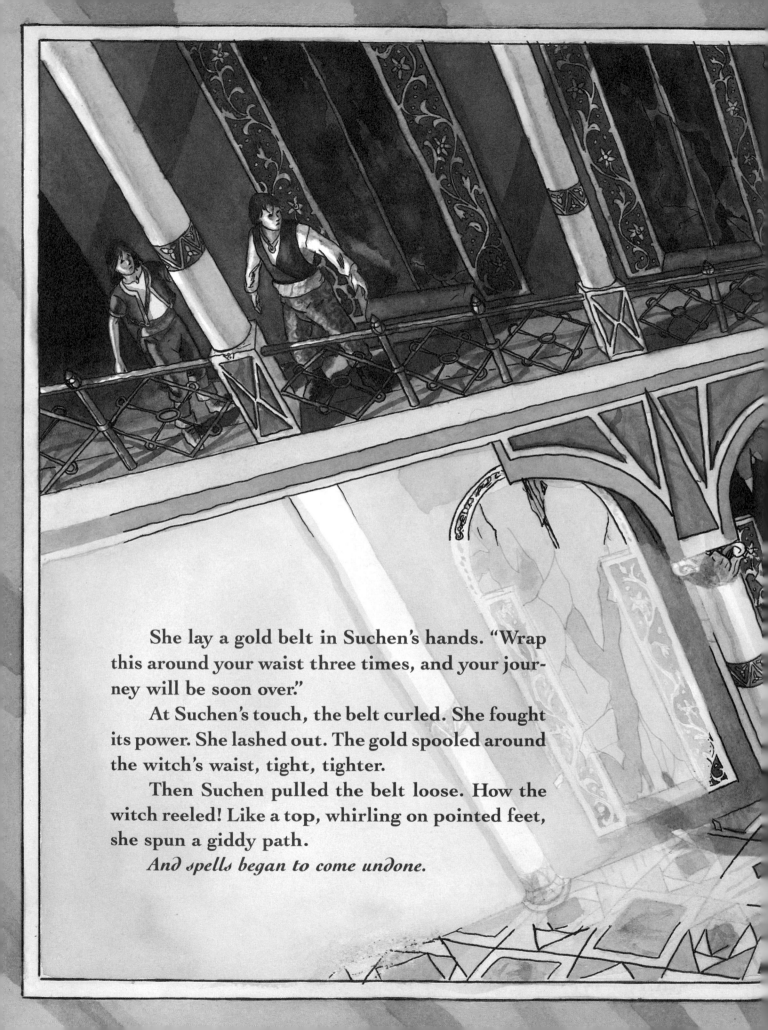

She lay a gold belt in Suchen's hands. "Wrap this around your waist three times, and your journey will be soon over."

At Suchen's touch, the belt curled. She fought its power. She lashed out. The gold spooled around the witch's waist, tight, tighter.

Then Suchen pulled the belt loose. How the witch reeled! Like a top, whirling on pointed feet, she spun a giddy path.

And spells began to come undone.

Suchen and the prince ran out of the hall.

From a well a snake rose and slid like a rope beneath them, carrying them over the castle wall. Two birds swooped down and lifted them high above the mountains, setting them down on a riverbank. A fish curved its back above the water and carried them to the other side.

The road home lay short and straight.

For seven days after there was singing and dancing and the sharing of tales as knights and explorers came home from Turnings.

The king presented golden medals to the mapmaker and his daughter. The prince gave Suchen a fine horse and a red cape,

which she wore on her next adventure.